HAMPTON YARDS

Also by Seth M. Siegel

Let There Be Water: Israel's Soloution for a Water-Starved World
Troubled Water: What's Wrong with What We Drink

Other People's Words

Other People's Words

WISDOM FOR AN INSPIRED AND PRODUCTIVE LIFE

SETH M. SIEGEL

ST.
MARTIN'S
PRESS
NEW YORK

First published in the United States by St. Martin's Press,
an imprint of St. Martin's Publishing Group

www.stmartins.com

Library of Congress Cataloging-in-Publication Data

Names: Siegel, Seth M., 1953– compiler.
Title: Other people's words : wisdom for an inspired and
   productive life / Seth M. Siegel.
Description: First edition. | New York : St. Martin's Press,
   2021. | Includes index.
Identifiers: LCCN 2020053524 | ISBN 9781250132567
   (hardcover) | ISBN 9781250132574 (ebook)
Subjects: LCSH: Commonplace books. | Conduct of life—
   Quotations, maxims, etc.
Classification: LCC PN6084.C556 O84 2021 | DDC 081—dc23
LC record available at https://lccn.loc.gov/2020053524

First Edition: 2021

10 9 8 7 6 5 4 3 2 1

For Rachel,
wife, best friend, wise partner, and
the kindest person I have ever known,
I dedicate this collection with
appreciation and love

Contents

SECTION 9 • THE DARK SIDE • 149

Anger · Anti-Semitism · Appeasement · Corruption · Cowardice · Dictators · Evil · Hate · The Holocaust · Imprisonment · Ingratitude · Neutrality · Pessimism and Pessimists · Prejudice · Racism · Rationalization · Slavery · Stupidity · Terrorism · Totalitarianism · Tragedy · War

SECTION 10 • OUR FRAGILE WORLD • 169

Civilization · Endangered Species · Environment · Food · Hunger · Nature · Poverty · Science · Technology · Water

SECTION 11 • DOING GOOD • 183

Charity · Community · Diplomacy · Education · Equality · Freedom · Human Rights · Immigrants · Justice and Injustice · Law · Learning · Morality · Peace · Progress · Public Service · Struggle · Teachers

Introduction

The day I started this quotations collection was also a day of culture shock. I was a member of a small delegation from my high school in a mostly Jewish and Black neighborhood in Queens, New York. We were visiting a high school in an affluent suburban community on Long Island that was unlike mine in more than ethnicity and race. While my school had crowded classrooms and three shifts to accommodate more than five thousand students, this one was amply spaced with small classes. As you might expect, it also had gorgeous athletic facilities, and even a parking lot for students who drove themselves to school.

What I remember most from the visit wasn't the disparity between our lives and theirs, but the social studies classroom where this collection began. Someone—probably the teacher—had mounted several powerfully worded quotations above the blackboard. Each was of the kind that might motivate a student to become an engaged citizen involved in some important cause. I can't say if any of the students were inspired by the ideas mounted on the wall, but I certainly was. Not carrying a notebook that day, I found a scrap of paper in my shirt pocket and copied down two of them.

The first of the quotations was attributed to eighteenth-century statesman and philosopher Edmund Burke. It was,

The only thing necessary for the triumph of evil is for good men to do nothing.

The second was equally dramatic. Soon after World War II, the anti-Nazi German theologian Martin Niemöller wrote,

They came first for the Communists, and I didn't speak up because I wasn't a Communist. Then they came for the Jews and I didn't speak up because I wasn't a Jew. Then they came for the trade unionists, and I didn't speak up because I wasn't a trade unionist. Then they came for me, and by that time there was no one left to speak up.

When I got home, I put the piece of paper into a drawer where I kept my T-shirts and socks. While I might have soon paid no attention to those two jotted-down sayings and the paper might have inched its way to the back of the dresser as forgotten keepsakes seem to do, instead, it somehow served as a catalyst. I began copying down other inspiring quotations and adding them to the drawer. From time to time, I'd take out all my scribbled notes and read through them, feeling wiser thanks to my contact with such profound ideas. But other than adding more bits of paper to the pile, it didn't then occur to me to do anything else with them.

Early in my second year of college, my connection to these scraps began to change. I started thinking of them as a collection worth tending. On a trip home, I put them all into a small box and brought them back to school. One rainy weekend, I typed out the many quotations I had copied down onto separate index cards, which I then organized alphabetically by categories I assigned to them.

In the months that followed, I found myself digging into my assigned class readings (and also into my own pleasure reading)

seeking more additions to the collection. The criteria for selection were that the quotation had to be brief and well phrased, and it also had to contain an idea that was new to me or that expressed, far better than I could, a thought I already had.

At the same time, I noticed the growing power of the collection as a whole over me. I realized I had begun internalizing the ideas in the collection, and a worldview—providing a framework for how I should live my life—began developing. Among other elements, this emerging worldview pushed me to stay away from distractions of the moment, to integrate my classroom learning into the larger lived world, and, amidst a dizzying range of choices, to figure out who I wanted to be. Not surprisingly, early additions to the collection spoke to each of these concerns.

For example, the importance of making good use of every minute was first conveyed to me by Benjamin Franklin's

Dost thou love life? Then do not squander time, for that's the stuff life is made of.

As for integrating what I was learning in class into how I lived my life, after reading a leaflet posted on a bulletin board that included advice from activist Tom Hayden, I took the flyer, cut out his words, and taped them to the desk in my dorm. Each day, I'd see and reread,

Do not study as a student, but as a person who is alive and who cares. Leave the isolated world of ideological fantasy, allow your ideas to become part of your living and your living to become part of your ideas.

And as for who I was and wanted to be, in a reading given to my creative writing class, I was moved by poet A. R. Ammons's thought that

You have your identity when you find out not what you can keep your mind on but what you can't keep your mind off.

While these quotations speak to behavior and personality, my collection wasn't limited to psychological insights or how best to motivate myself. I also began collecting comments on an array of topics like justice, nature, war, photography, and politics. As with the collected wisdom directed at my interior life, these selections helped me to understand and talk about a variety of fields, often also contributing to some part of my developing worldview.

In a political philosophy class, for example, I stumbled on an observation by the ancient Greek writer Plutarch that

They are wrong who think that politics is like an ocean voyage or a military campaign, something to be done with some particular end in view, something which leaves off as soon as that end is reached. It is not a public chore, to be got over with. It is a way of life.

Beyond the plain meaning of the words, Plutarch's advice also served to encourage my then still-evolving work ethic and to focus me on the need to take a long view while staying attentive to what's important in the moment.

Alas, college doesn't last forever, but the benefit from pursuing a moral center and a coherent worldview does. In the years since college—which have included graduate study in international relations, law school, working as a lawyer, falling in love and marrying, starting a business career, helping to raise a family, serving as a volunteer in several not-for-profit organizations, and writing two books—the collection has continued to grow, as has its influence on me. Again, a few examples.

As a working person trying to build a business and to maximize my family's assets, I often needed a reminder to take time to focus on self-improvement and personal fulfillment. A short saying from a nineteenth-century essayist and critic that I've repeated countless times has especially served as that reminder. It is

Life is not a having and a getting, but a being and a becoming. (*Matthew Arnold*)

I've since sold my company and departed from it. For many years, I've mostly spent my days writing, speaking, and doing volunteer communal service—all of which have given me a different kind of joy and fulfillment than I found in the world of business. But it doesn't mean that I never look back at what I left behind. When I speak with former colleagues who are continuing to attain ever-greater financial success, I sometimes wonder if I should have continued on as an executive. Matthew Arnold's words remain a constant companion, reminding me that the path I've chosen is right for me and urging me to continue on it.

But the potential for backsliding into feeling insecure or thinking more is needed has also been beaten back with regular reference to another, yet older, insight. Quite by chance, one wintry Saturday afternoon, I came across a piece of ancient Jewish wisdom that—as with the Matthew Arnold quotation—also reinforces the decision I had made to change the focus of my life. It is

Who is the wealthy one? The person satisfied with his lot in life. (*Ben Zoma*)

The simple message of these wise words is that it's a fool's errand to think that having more is the way to be happy. Ben Zoma reminds me that we are rich when we feel content with what we have.

As it turned out, I even felt the influence of this collection while writing this introduction. I spent weeks writing and polishing what I thought would serve as a wonderful opening essay for the book. I sent it to my friend, Dan Polisar, who had helped found a college and, of more relevance, is a terrific editor. He told me my orientation was all wrong, that I should get rid of what I had written and start all over with a different approach. With some disappointment, I saw he was right, and spent another few weeks writing a different introduction. I sent it to him again, expecting an admiring thumbs-up. Instead, he said that it was closer, but still not right. As I was about to start finding excuses to ignore what he had to say and go with what I had in hand, I remembered a quotation in the collection:

The trouble with most of us is that we'd rather be ruined by praise than saved by criticism. (*Norman Vincent Peale*)

So, I went back to the keyboard, frustrated yet again, and grateful to him that he saved me (I hope) with his criticism.

* * *

There's no question that I've been the greatest beneficiary of this collection. But I haven't been the only one helped by it. Over the years, friends, business associates, and the children of both, have come to me for personal or professional advice. Though I lack training as a therapist or career counselor, what I bring to these conversations is not only my own life experiences, but also the time-tested and inspiring insights of the hundreds of wise advisers whose thoughts fill my collection— and my mind.

Five or six years ago, for example, a friend told me he was

planning on quitting the board of trustees of a charity on which he had served for many years because he had been repeatedly passed over as the organization's annual dinner honoree. After reminding him of his great belief in the mission of the group, I shared a favorite quotation from Robert Woodruff, Coca-Cola's longtime president who turned the company's namesake beverage into a worldwide brand.

There is no limit to what a man can do or where he can go if he doesn't mind who gets the credit.

My friend has stayed with the organization to this day.

A man in his early thirties whom I met through my communal volunteer work was a bright executive with great potential. He told me that he dreamed of starting his own business, but was afraid of the consequences of failure for his young family and his reputation. He also told me had enough savings to cover a few years of living expenses. I shared British psychologist John Bowlby's advice that

Life is best organized as a series of daring ventures from a secure base.

A few days after that discussion, he resigned from his job and started a business that is still going strong more than ten years later. He has often given me credit for his making that decision.

In many settings where people are frittering away their time, especially when larger opportunities are before them, I'll quote the author of *The Lord of the Rings,* J. R. R. Tolkien, and say,

All we have to decide is what to do with the time that is given us.

Or when people tell me they are unhappy and are thinking of moving somewhere they don't know very well with the hope that a change of scenery will turbocharge their life, I've often shared journalist Morton Kondracke's advice that

If you're not happy where you are, you won't be happy where you aren't.

Or when people complain that they have been unlucky because this or that opportunity fell through, I enjoy reciting novelist Cormac McCarthy's fatalistic advice that

You never know what worse luck your bad luck has saved you from.

Or when people say that they just want to be happy, I may pass along former First Lady Eleanor Roosevelt's reply to a similar comment, and say,

Happiness is not a goal, it is a by-product of a life well lived.

And when people tell me that they have a plan for something, as if the plan is a bridge to a destination and not just a first step on a long road fraught with difficulties to be overcome, I never tire of quoting boxing heavyweight champion Mike Tyson's practical insight,

Everyone's got a plan until they get punched in the mouth.

Since the publication of my first book, I've often been contacted by writers and would-be writers asking for advice. Depending on the situation, there is a good chance I'll quote one of several ideas that have guided me along my writing career, including,

The hardest thing about writing is writing.
(*Nora Ephron*)

Your last piece is never going to write your next one for you. (*John McPhee*)

You learn to write by writing, not thinking about it.
Don't wait for the Muse to tap you on the shoulder.
(*Frank Herbert*)

At no time, though, has my collection had a greater impact than the interaction I had with one public figure, a man of great integrity whom I admired and who decided to run for high elective office. I offered—and he accepted—my help with ideas for his campaign, along with fundraising and speechwriting. I soon had daily contact with the candidate and his staff, and I grew to like and admire him even more as the campaign moved forward.

Unexpectedly, a leading newspaper ran a front-page story that called his honesty into question. The article called him out over a handful of embellishments in stories he had told that were unrelated to the high office he was pursuing. Because of the stature of both the newspaper and the candidate, the story was picked up by television stations and other newspapers throughout his state. The fast-traveling news humiliated him and drained his self-confidence.

The next day, he told me he would be withdrawing from the race. He said that the article gave his opponent ammunition to run withering attack ads, and would require him to endure months of character assassination. Even if he won, his good name would be permanently tarnished.

I was sure that I wasn't his first phone call and whatever arguments I had to persuade him to stay in the race, he'd likely have already heard from others. But I had something no one else had: a collection of wise thoughts that were relevant to a wide range of situations, including his. In the course of our conversation, I offered several quotations that I hoped would raise his spirits and give him courage for what was sure to be some very hard months ahead.

If what the newspaper reported was correct, he had taken liberties and exaggerated elements about his personal experiences. But there was no doubt that the underlying stories were based on real episodes in which he had shown intelligence or demonstrated courage. Given this narrow set of facts—that is, of real stories somewhat puffed up—I offered a quotation from *East of Eden,* one of the masterworks from Nobel Prize–winning author John Steinbeck,

The difference between a lie and a story is that a story utilizes the trappings and appearance of truth for the interest of the listener as well as of the teller. A story has in it neither gain nor loss. But a lie is a device for profit or escape.

Yes, he had embellished some stories about his life, but he wasn't giving testimony at a deposition or a trial. He was speaking the way normal people do. And if he did embellish the stories, so what? After all, "a story has in it neither gain nor loss." The newspaper could imply he was a liar, but he wasn't one. He could rest assured that he didn't have some terrible character flaw and could stop beating himself up.

I also reminded him of something said by nineteenth-century British prime minister Benjamin Disraeli,

Today they blacken your character, tomorrow they blacken [that is, shine] your boots.

Today, I acknowledged, your life is miserable, and maybe the next few months will be, as well. But come November, the election brings this all to an end, and either way—and especially if you are elected—this will largely be forgotten by everyone (but you). If you win, people will clamor to have your attention. Soon, they will figuratively be shining your shoes.

As we were wrapping up our conversation, I asked my friend, a non-practicing Protestant who was not much of a Bible reader, if he was familiar with the Book of Esther. He was not. I told the story of how an order for the annihilation of all the Jews in the Persian kingdom had been issued. Queen Esther, a Jew, had until that point hidden her religious identity. While she wanted to stop the massacres, she feared that if she revealed her heritage to the king and asked to call off the planned mass murder that she would die. Her uncle, Mordechai, comes to her, with a plea and a rebuke, saying,

Do not imagine that you will be able to escape in the King's palace any more than the rest of the Jews. For if you persist in keeping silent at a time like this, relief and deliverance will come to the Jews from some other place, while you and your father's house will perish. And who knows whether it was just for such a time that you attained the royal position!

Before hanging up, I reprised Mordechai's message, and said, "Who knows whether it was for just such a time that you are running for this office."

That evening, he called me and asked me to read him the Steinbeck and Mordechai quotations, along with a few others, once more. I took that as a hopeful sign.

The next morning, he got in touch again to say that he had decided to stay in the race. That November, he was elected to the United States Senate. At his swearing-in ceremony, he reminded me of our long conversation and of the ideas I had shared during one of the darkest days of his life.

* * *

Having seen the power of this collection in my own life and in those of family and friends, I believe it can also be of benefit to many others beyond my circle. Even so, I hesitated when the publisher of my earlier books suggested I gather my quotations and share them with a broader audience.

First, some of what is here is very personal. I wondered what inferences people who don't know me might draw from the many quotations included that address courage, competition, integrity, or persistence in one way or another.

Similarly, while close friends might have known about my painful relationships with certain family members, I asked myself if some entries here hint at more than I might want to reveal, such as Nobel Prize–winner Isaac Bashevis Singer's observation that

There are secrets that the heart cannot reveal to the lips.

Or writer Robert Anderson's acute insight that

Death ends a life, but it does not end a relationship, which struggles on in the survivor's mind towards some resolution which it may never find.

Second, I worried that readers might see this book as too much ego at work, especially in my thinking that others would care to see all of this. After all, I include Pulitzer Prize–winning composer Ned Rorem's funny, but true, comment that

All art is egocentric. Beethoven assumes that you want to listen to those goddamn symphonies of his.

In publishing this collection, I assume that someone wants to read these [expletive deleted] quotations.

And related to that, I was concerned that in sharing this collection I could be accused of presumptuousness or even arrogance. Notwithstanding the inclusion of some truly terrible people here, I present many great thinkers as my advisers, confidants, and sources of inspiration. Citing such individuals and presenting myself as a conduit for their timeless ideas might unintentionally reflect a sense of self-importance.

In the end, despite these misgivings, I decided to share my collection because I've seen the value it has brought to so many others. While I served as the collector, curator, and organizer of what is here, I realized, my role is secondary. In the end, each of the nearly 1,200 quotations from about 750 sources speaks for itself.

To promote accessibility, I've divided the book into eleven sections, each of which focuses on a separate general theme such as our interior lives, important relationships, doing good, creativity, politics, money, and even the dark side of life. Each section is further divided by thematically related categories, and those categories have from two to twenty quotations in them. While the items in each section are connected conceptually, all of the quotations within each category are—with one or two exceptions—separate and independent thoughts. Although few quotations contradict others, many approach the same idea from different perspectives. That isn't redundancy, but nuance, reflecting the reality that life is complex and that there are often several ways of looking at the same issue.

If your experience with this collection encourages you to start a quotations collection of your own, I hope you do. If so, you can follow my example and grab anything that inspires, amuses, motivates, or excites you that you think you might like to see again. Feel free to take anything in this book that has caught your eye to help you get started. Collecting quotations—and using them—is the only place in the world of words where no one is ever accused of plagiarism.

If you do start collecting, also be ready to delete whatever loses its power over you. The point of collecting quotations isn't to amass the largest number of examples possible, but to have intellectual companions who can travel with you through life—and no one wants a tedious travel mate whose insights become stale. Since most of the selections I've chosen were fascinating to me when I first encountered them, a significant majority remain intriguing and interesting to me many years after I first happened upon them. But there are also many I once loved that have been cut. Ironically, given what those first two selections from that social studies classroom set in motion, neither of them has survived within my collection. I came to see both as melodramatic and even untrue without some qualification. My gratitude for getting me started notwithstanding, removing them from the collection was an easy decision.

The journey from that Long Island high school to today has been a long one in years, ideas, activities—and quotations collected. I've experienced great joy, with disappointments mostly kept at bay by luck and with a perspective that keeps me focused on what is most important in life: family, service to community, self-respect, and moving forward in pursuit of meaningful achievements. While my wife—to whom I dedicate this volume—is more responsible for that happy life than anyone or anything else, having a worldview created in large part by other people's words to guide me has played an essential role. I hope this collection inspires you in a happier, more fulfilling life, too.

Note to the Reader

There are many ways to read, enjoy, and benefit from this book. You may want to randomly read here and there, or you may prefer to take a more structured approach. It's your book and you should feel comfortable accessing this collection in any way that is most comfortable and enriching for you.

Some who read an earlier, privately printed version of this edition have told me that they would read quotations from the book each night before bed. Someone else told me she took her copy on car trips with friends, with the book being passed around with each (nondriver) picking an entry as the basis for a conversation that would continue until the next quotation was selected. Similarly, a man with teenaged children read a quotation each evening at the start of dinner to prompt a family conversation. A clergyman I know who received a copy told me he would pull quotations out and work them into his sermons, and another friend had me send him several copies so that he could hand each one out to family members as they graduated from high school or college.

Regardless of how you choose to engage with this collection, I'd like to think that you'll get several important benefits. In addition to being exposed to new ideas, many of the quotations here have the potential to provoke valuable self-exploration. As I describe in the introduction, my frequent rereading of the quotations here led to my developing a comprehensive worldview and personal philosophy that serve to guide me on matters large and small. If you repeatedly return to the many entries here, it may do the same for you.

For ease of use and for coherence, I have organized this book into sections and categories. In so doing, I may have also created a potential problem. By putting a quotation into a section or category, I may, unintentionally, bias your engagement with the quotation due to that editorial overlay. Ideally, my choice of section or category should not affect your reaction to what you have read.

Also, for nearly every quotation, only the author of the quotation is provided. Where needed for context, such as if the quotation is a line of dialogue from a novel or a film, more information is provided. If you are eager to know the origins of a quotation, you can probably find it with an internet search. If that fails, feel free to contact me.

You will likely notice that I have omitted honorifics, titles, and other descriptive information about the authors of the quotations. Although there are twenty former U.S. presidents whose quotations appear here as well as prime ministers and other elected officials, judges, clergy—and even a few people on whom sainthood has been bestowed—nearly all are identified only by their names. An exception was made when the person is only known with their appended title, such as Princess Diana or Mother Teresa, or when the person's title is relevant to an enhanced engagement with a quotation, such as in the case of a senator describing his cynically voting with special interests while pretending to believe otherwise, or a congressman referring to congressmen as idiots, or the first woman to join the U.S. Supreme Court speaking about women and that court. Except for these very few entries, I hope that each quotation stands on its own without a call to authority offered by an esteemed title.

It is important to me to give proper credit to the person who actually created the quotation selected. It is often the case that people have inadvertently or otherwise made use of an idea or an exact quotation from someone else without having given credit. The more famous, later popularizer of a quotation sometimes comes to be thought of as the creator. Wherever possible, I give credit to the actual author of the quotation. Related to that, in a few rare instances, even lots of detective work can't offer assurance as to the author of the quotation. For those quotations, I've indicated the lack of certainty by the notation "attributed, not confirmed."

Some of the people quoted here are unsavory or controversial individuals. Inclusion in this collection does not imply respect for the person who said it or endorsement of any body of that person's work or ideas beyond the one that is quoted. Even so, I apologize if you are offended by my inclusion of people who are clearly not role models.

It would be impossible to not notice the change in language during the course of the time I've been collecting. The word "men" is used by writers and speakers to mean "people" in quotations throughout the collection. In almost every case, the quotation would be unimpaired if the gender-neutral term had been used. I've left these otherwise admirable quotations in the collection while also acknowledging here the more generally inclusive, and fairer, use of language today.

Finally, as much as I enjoy sharing quotations, I also like seeing what other people are collecting, whether it is a single quotation on a refrigerator door or a file larger than mine. Please contact me at **www.SethMSiegel.com** and share your quotations—and your comments.

SECTION 1

Our Inner Selves

"The greater part of our happiness or misery depends on our dispositions and not on our circumstances."
Martha Washington

"A soul isn't something a person is born with but something that must be built, by effort and error, study and love."
Chad Harbach

CHARACTER

"Character may be manifested in the great moments, but it is made in the small ones."
Winston Churchill

"People, even the wicked, are much more naïve and simple-hearted than we suppose. And we ourselves are, too."
Fyodor Dostoyevsky

"Important events—whether serious, happy or unfortunate—do not change a man's soul, they merely bring it into relief, just as a strong gust of wind reveals the true shape of a tree when it blows off all its leaves. Such events highlight what is hidden in the shadows."
Irene Nemirovsky

"Whoever thinks that he alone possesses intelligence, the gift of eloquence, he and no one else, and character too . . . such men, I tell you, spread them open—you will find them empty."
Sophocles

"Rudeness is the weak man's imitation of strength."
Eric Hoffer

"The true measure of a man is how he treats someone who can do him absolutely no good."
Samuel Johnson

"Character is destiny."
   Heraclitus

CONFORMISM

"Be orderly and regular in your life, like a bourgeois, so that you may be wild and original in your work."
   Gustave Flaubert

"What I realized much later, paradoxically, is that by trying to fit in, I was strengthening the culture that made me feel like I didn't fit in."
   Melinda Gates

"The reward for conformity was that everyone liked you but yourself."
   Rita Mae Brown

"We're all pretty bizarre. Some of us are just better at hiding it."
   John Hughes

COURAGE

"Courage is rightly esteemed the first of human qualities because it is the quality that guarantees all others."
   Winston Churchill

"One man with courage makes a majority."
   Andrew Jackson (attributed, not confirmed)

"Courage is resistance to fear, mastery of fear—not absence of fear."
   Mark Twain

"Strength and courage are not things that happen to us; they are choices we make. They are the heavenly markers by which we set the course for our lives."

Bryceson Tenold

CYNICISM

"Cynicism is a dangerous disease, a cancer of the soul. Often, we don't know we have it, until it's too late, until part of us has died. It's also contagious."

Daniel Gordis

"Cynicism is often a product of disappointed idealism—of naïveté being crushed by reality."

James Taranto

"If everybody always lies to you, the consequence is not that you believe the lies, but rather that nobody believes anything any longer."

Hannah Arendt

"I try to be cynical, but it's hard to keep up."

Lily Tomlin

DISAPPOINTMENT

"Disappointment is the gap between expectation and reality."

Mordehai Mironi

"Nowadays, I don't have expectations [of her], and this way she beats them all."

Jodi Picoult, in *My Sister's Keeper*

"There is a special form of disappointment when you feel disappointed even after you expected to be disappointed."
Sam Siegel

ENTHUSIASM

"Sometimes the appetite comes with the eating."
Israeli saying

"Once you lose your enthusiasm, you lose your integrity. And once you lose your integrity, you're a con man."
Russ Reid

"Fires can't be made with dead embers, nor can enthusiasm be stirred by spiritless men. Enthusiasm in our daily work lightens effort and turns even labor into pleasant tasks."
James Baldwin

FAITH

"If gods exist, you have nothing to fear in taking leave of mankind, for they will not let you come to harm. But if there are no gods, or if they have no concern with mortal affairs, what is life to me in a world devoid of gods or devoid of Providence?"
Marcus Aurelius

"When a man stops believing in God, he doesn't then believe in nothing, he believes anything."
G. K. Chesterton

"O Lord, if there is a Lord, save my soul, if I have a soul."
Ernest Renan

HAPPINESS

"The greater part of our happiness or misery depends on our dispositions and not on our circumstances."
Martha Washington

"Happiness is not a goal. It is a by-product of a life well lived."
Eleanor Roosevelt

"A man has happiness if he possesses three things—those whom he loves and who love him in turn, confidence in the worth and continued existence of the group of which he is a part, and last of all, a truth by which he may order his being."
Milton Steinberg

"We're all searching for happiness; we're all living lives that are different and yet the same."
Anne Frank

"If you're not happy where you are, you won't be happy where you aren't."
Morton Kondracke

"There is a kind of happiness in unhappiness, if it is the right unhappiness."
Jonathan Franzen

"I'm always happy. Sometimes I just forget."
Jennifer Egan

"Each of us has his own rhythm of suffering."
Roland Barthes

"They say it is better to be poor and happy than rich and miserable, but how about a compromise like moderately rich and just moody?"
Princess Diana

"The goal of psychoanalysis is to turn neurotic misery into everyday unhappiness."
Sigmund Freud

"Risk-taking, trust and serendipity are key ingredients of joy. Without risk, nothing new ever happens. Without trust, fear creeps in. Without serendipity, there are no surprises."
Rita Golden Gelman

"What a wonderful life I've had! I only wish I'd realized it sooner."
Sidonie-Gabrielle Colette

HONESTY

"A man who will lie for me will lie to me."
Arthur Morgan

"All cruel people describe themselves as paragons of frankness."
Tennessee Williams

"You can't pay off innocent people."
Thomas P. Puccio

"Sometimes a lie is used in kindness, but I don't believe it ever works kindly. The quick pain of truth can pass away, but the slow, eating agony of a lie is never lost."
John Steinbeck

"Confession is good for the soul but bad for the reputation."
  Mark Twain

"Real integrity is doing the right thing, knowing that nobody's
going to know whether you did it or not."
  Oprah Winfrey

HUMILITY

"You can boast about anything if it's all you have. Maybe the
less you have, the more you are required to boast."
  John Steinbeck

"True humility is not thinking less of yourself; it is thinking of
yourself less."
  Rick Warren

"The only true wisdom is in knowing you know nothing."
  Socrates

"I am often in error, but never in doubt."
  William Safire

IDENTITY

"Take what you do seriously. But don't take yourself seriously."
  Jeff Garlin

"We are what we pretend to be, so we must be careful about
what we pretend to be."
  Kurt Vonnegut

"Just because one is born in a stable does not make one a horse."

Arthur Wellesley

"I did not, as hypocrites do, have one real face and various false ones. I had several faces only because I was young and did not know who I was or who I wanted to be. But the difference between all these faces frightened me; none of them seemed to fit properly, and I changed from one to the other clumsily and haphazardly."

Milan Kundera

"Do I contradict myself? Very well, then I contradict myself, I am large, I contain multitudes."

Walt Whitman

"The most important thing to remember is this: to be ready at any moment to give up what you are for what you might become."

W. E. B. Du Bois

"You have your identity when you find out not what you can keep your mind on but what you can't keep your mind off."

A. R. Ammons

"A soul isn't something a person is born with but something that must be built, by effort and error, study and love."

Chad Harbach

"The way to know me is to know my work; I am my work."

Mother Teresa

"You are what you love, not what loves you."

Charlie Kaufman

"Beauty begins the moment you decide to be yourself."
  Coco Chanel

"If I am not for me, who will be? If I am only for myself, what am I? And if not now, when?"
  Hillel, in *Teachings of the Fathers*

"How can you hate all you have come from and not hate yourself?"
  Anne Michaels

"Build your life as if it were a work of art."
  Abraham Joshua Heschel

INSECURITY

"I don't think I ever met a superachiever who wasn't insecure to some degree. A superachiever is somebody that's never satisfied."
  Ted Turner

"Those who need no introduction crave it the most."
  Henry A. Kissinger

"The problem with being a relentless competitor is that you can always feel badly about something."
  Victor Schwartz

KINDNESS

"When I was young, I admired clever people. Now that I am old, I admire kind people."
  Abraham Joshua Heschel

"Kindness is in our power, but fondness is not."
   Samuel Johnson

"The simplest acts of kindness are more powerful than a thousand heads bowed in prayer."
   Mohandas Gandhi

LONELINESS

"We're born alone, we live alone, we die alone. Only through our love and friendship can we create the illusion for the moment that we're not alone."
   Orson Welles

"No technological achievements can mitigate the disappointment of modern man, his loneliness, his feeling of inferiority, and his fear of war, revolution and terror. Not only has our generation lost faith in Providence, but also in man himself, in his institutions and often in those who are nearest to him."
   Isaac Bashevis Singer, in his Nobel Prize lecture

"Solitude is fine but you need someone to tell that solitude is fine."
   Honoré de Balzac

"Homesickness is like any other sickness. At first, you feel like you're going to die, and then you get over it. And the sickness moves on to torment someone else."
   Nick Hornby

"The most terrible poverty is loneliness, and the feeling of being unloved."
   Mother Teresa

PASSION

"You have to be burning with an idea, or a problem, or a wrong that you want to right. If you're not passionate enough from the start, you'll never stick it out."
Steve Jobs

"Do what you love, and you'll never work a day in your life."
George Burns (attributed, not confirmed)

"Passion is one great force that unleashes creativity, because if you're passionate about something then you're more willing to take risks."
Yo-Yo Ma

"The most beautiful makeup for a woman is passion. But cosmetics are easier to buy."
Yves Saint-Laurent

"He who has a why to live can bear with almost any how."
Friedrich Nietzsche

"Passion will move men beyond themselves, beyond their shortcomings, beyond their failures."
Joseph Campbell

PRAISE

"Anything in any way beautiful derives its beauty from itself and asks nothing beyond itself. Praise is no part of it, for nothing is made worse or better by praise."
Marcus Aurelius

"The silence that comes after a lifetime of applause can be particularly deafening."
Dan Le Batard

"I don't like the idea of awards for artistic things. They're not created for the purpose of competition; they're made to fulfill an artistic itch and hopefully entertain. I'm not interested in any group's pronunciamento as to which is the best film of the year, or the best book, or the Most Valuable Player."
Woody Allen

"There is no limit to what a man can do or where he can go if he doesn't mind who gets the credit."
Robert W. Woodruff

"Flattery is one of life's best lubricants."
Philip Galanes

RELIGION

"Sensible men are all of the same religion."
Benjamin Disraeli

"It is in the nature of man to like what he is familiar with and in which he has been brought up, and that he fears anything alien. The plurality of religions and their mutual intolerance result from the fact that people remain faithful to the education they received."
Maimonides

"No religion is an island."
Abraham Joshua Heschel

"My religion is very simple. My religion is kindness."
Dalai Lama

SELF-CONFIDENCE

"There is no 'I' in team, but there is an 'I' in win."
Michael Jordan

"I am larger, better than I thought. I did not know I held so much goodness."
Walt Whitman

"Stand for something or you will fall for anything. Today's mighty oak is yesterday's nut that held its ground."
Rosa Parks

"Fashion is not necessarily about labels. It's not about brands. It's about something else that comes from within you."
Ralph Lauren

"I never cut class. I loved getting A's, I liked being smart. I liked being on time. I thought being smart is cooler than anything in the world."
Michelle Obama

SELF-RESPECT

"The most luxurious possession, the richest treasure anybody has, is his personal dignity."
Jackie Robinson

"Self-esteem comes from achievements. Not from lax standards and false praise."

Condoleezza Rice

"Success, wealth, and celebrity, gained and kept for private interest, are small things. But sacrifice for a cause greater than self-interest, and you invest your life with the eminence of that cause, and your self-respect is assured."

John McCain

"No one can make you feel inferior without your consent."

Eleanor Roosevelt

SILENCE

"Clever talk is absolutely worthless. All you do in the process is lose yourself. And to lose yourself is a sin. One has to be able to crawl completely inside oneself, like a tortoise."

Hermann Hesse

"We have two ears and one mouth so that we can listen twice as much as we speak."

Epictetus

"The silence of two people is deeper than the silence of one."

Elie Wiesel

"Nowhere can man find a quieter or more untroubled retreat than in his own soul."

Marcus Aurelius

"Sometimes one creates a dynamic impression by saying some-

thing, and sometimes one creates as significant an impression by remaining silent."
Dalai Lama

TRAUMA AND RESILIENCE

"When you come out of the storm, you won't be the same person who walked in."
Haruki Murakami

"There's only so many traumas a person can withstand until they take to the streets and start screaming."
Woody Allen, in Blue Jasmine

"That which does not kill us, makes us stronger."
Friedrich Nietzsche

"You may encounter many defeats, but you must not be defeated."
Maya Angelou

"Our greatest glory is not in never falling, but in rising every time we fall."
Confucius

TRUTH

"Telling the truth is a skill. Those who don't do it habitually lose the ability."
David Brooks

"You know what's so good about the truth? Everyone knows what it is however long they've lived without it. No one forgets the truth. They just get better at lying."

Justin Haythe

"But if the truth causes scandal, then it is better a scandal arise than that the truth be abandoned."

Gregory I

"Those who are eager to burn the mists of myth from the public mind should pause to consider what may fill the void. It is not adequate to simply say: 'The truth shall make us free.' Various truths, at different times and places, have various effects, not all of them nice."

George F. Will

"We may accept truth no matter how bitter its consequence but we do not necessarily honor the truth sayer."

Louis Nizer

"The most dangerous of all moral dilemmas: When we are obliged to conceal the truth in order to help the truth be victorious."

Dag Hammarskjöld

"All great truths begin as blasphemies."

George Bernard Shaw

"The half-truths of one generation tend at times to perpetuate themselves as the whole truths of another, when constant repetition brings it about that qualifications, taken once for granted, are disregarded or forgotten."

Benjamin Cardozo

"Poetic truth is like poetic license where one breaks grammatical rules for effect. Better to break the rule than lose the effect. Poetic truth lies just a little; it bends the actual truth in order to highlight what it believes is a larger and more important truth."

Shelby Steele

"The difference between a lie and a story is that a story utilizes the trappings and appearance of truth for the interest of the listener as well as of the teller. A story has in it neither gain nor loss. But a lie is a device for profit or escape."

John Steinbeck

"When you want to help people, you tell them the truth. When you want to help yourself, you tell them what they want to hear."

Thomas Sowell

SECTION 2

Becoming Our Best

"How we spend our days is, of course, how we spend our lives."
Annie Dillard

"A great flame follows a little spark."
Dante

ADVERSITY

"Ease destroys bravery, while trouble and concern create strength."
Maimonides

"It is difficulties that show what men are."
Epictetus

"The ultimate measure of a man is not where he stands in moments of comfort and convenience, but where he stands at times of challenge and controversy."
Martin Luther King, Jr.

"I have been bent and broken, but hopefully into a better shape."
Charles Dickens, in *Great Expectations*

"Even against the greatest of odds, there is something in the human spirit—a magic blend of skill, faith and valor—that can lift men from certain defeat to incredible victory."
Walter Lord

AMBITION

"For what shall it profit a man if he shall gain the whole world and lose his own soul?"
Mark 8:36

"Ambition is one of the more ungovernable passions of the human heart. The love of power is insatiable and uncontrollable."
John Adams

"Achievement is almost always measured as a fraction of ambition."
Bret Stephens

"People with excessive ambition are unwise to reveal that fact while they are still unimportant."
Jerzy Andrzejewski

CHALLENGES

"There is never time in the future in which we will work out our salvation. The challenge is in the moment; the time is always now."
James Baldwin

"If things seem under control, you're not going fast enough."
Mario Andretti

"You have to motivate yourself with challenges. That's how you know you're still alive. Once you start doing only what you've proven you can do, you're on the road to death."
Jerry Seinfeld

"When life becomes an extended picnic, with nothing of importance to do, ideas of greatness become an irritant."
Charles Murray

"Few things are difficult, but everything takes time."
Rachel Ringler

"If you can't go through an obstacle, go around it. Water does."
Margaret Atwood

"Never let the fear of striking out get in your way."
Babe Ruth

"There will always be more problems than solutions; more to be done than has been done; more quests than conquests. The game is lost only when we stop trying."
Mario Cuomo

"Hard is not hopeless."
David Petraeus

"You never know how far you can run unless you run."
Penny Chenery

CRITICISM

"Critics are our friends, they show us our faults."
Benjamin Franklin

"The trouble with most of us is that we'd rather be ruined by praise than saved by criticism."
Norman Vincent Peale

"Let me never fall into the vulgar mistake of dreaming that I am persecuted whenever I am contradicted."
Ralph Waldo Emerson

"Honest and earnest criticism from those whose interests are most nearly touched—criticism of writers by readers, of

government by those governed, of leaders by those led—this is the soul of democracy and the safeguard of modern society."
  W. E. B. Du Bois

"Nobody kicks a dead dog."
  Dale Carnegie

"I've been all over the world and I've never seen a statue of a critic."
  Leonard Bernstein

EATING

"Hunger is the best sauce in the world."
  Miguel de Cervantes

"Nothing tastes as good as skinny feels."
  Kate Moss

"Eat to live, not live to eat."
  Jean-Baptiste Molière

"Eating should be fun. Don't be afraid of your food."
  Gil Hovav

"You don't have to cook fancy or complicated masterpieces— just good food from fresh ingredients."
  Julia Child

"Eat food. Not too much. Mostly plants."
  Michael Pollan

EXERCISE

"The doctor of the future will give no medicine, but will involve the patient in the proper use of food, fresh air, and exercise."
Thomas Edison

"Not less than two hours a day should be devoted to exercise, and the weather should be little regarded."
Thomas Jefferson

"An early-morning walk is a blessing for the whole day."
Henry David Thoreau

"Training gives us an outlet for suppressed energies created by stress and thus tones the spirit just as exercise conditions the body."
Arnold Schwarzenegger

"Just do it."
Nike slogan

FEAR

"Fear is stronger than compassion."
Yoel Esteron

"Turbulence does not kill airplanes. But it agitates the mind and sets it thinking about the things—freakish mostly—that do kill planes."
Verlyn Klinkenborg

"Fear is an insidious and deadly thing. It can warp judgment, freeze reflexes, breed mistakes. Worse, it's contagious."
Jimmy Stewart

HABIT

"Habit is habit, and not to be flung out of the window . . . but coaxed downstairs a step at a time."
Mark Twain

"Chains of habit are too light to be felt until they are too heavy to be broken."
Warren Buffett

"Don't say you can't give up drinking. It's easy. I've done it a thousand times."
W. C. Fields

LEGACY

"Every institution is the lengthened shadow of one man."
Ralph Waldo Emerson

"The evil that men do lives after them; the good is oft interred with their bones."
William Shakespeare

"All predominant power seems for a time invincible but, in fact, it is transient. The question is: What do you leave behind?"
Tony Blair

"I'd rather it be said that I lived usefully than that I died wealthily."
Benjamin Franklin

"My life is my message."
Mohandas Gandhi

MISTAKES

"The man who makes no mistakes does not usually make anything."
E. J. Phelps

"Nothing sharpens my focus like a mistake."
Melinda Gates

"There is no such thing as a mistake. There is what you do and what you don't do."
Alvin Sargent

"If I had to live my life again, I'd make the same mistakes, only sooner."
Tallulah Bankhead

OLD AGE

"Old age is always fifteen years older than I am."
Bernard M. Baruch

"Old age is like a plane flying through a storm. Once you're aboard, there's nothing you can do. You can't stop the plane, you can't stop the storm, you can't stop time. So one might as well accept it calmly, wisely."

Golda Meir

"By a certain age, one's mistrust is so exquisitely refined that one is unwilling to believe anybody."

Philip Roth, in *The Human Stain*

"None are so old as those who have outlived enthusiasm."

Henry David Thoreau

"How did you get so old? Was it all at once, in a day, or did you peter out bit by bit? When did you stop having parties? Did everyone else get old too, or was it just you? When did you swim your last laps? Do your bones hurt? Did you know this was coming and hide that you know, or did it ambush you from behind?"

Jennifer Egan, in *A Visit from the Goon Squad*

"We imagine that we change our opinions or our personalities or our taste in music as we ripen, often feeling that we are betraying our younger selves. Really, though, our bodies just change . . . We can't help it. The chemistry has altered. This means that some things that were once present to us become invisible, go off the screen; the compensation is that new things swim into view."

Louis Menand

"Every man desires to live long, but no man would be old."

Jonathan Swift

"Old age isn't a battle; old age is a massacre."

Philip Roth, in *Everyman*

"At night, you can see stars you can't see in the day. With age, you get insights you don't have when you are younger."

Ted Comet

PERSISTENCE

"Nothing in the world can take the place of persistence. Talent will not; nothing is more common than unsuccessful men with talent. Genius will not; unrewarded genius is almost a proverb. Education will not; the world is full of educated derelicts. Persistence and determination alone are omnipotent. The slogan 'Press on' has solved and always will solve the problems of the human race."
   Calvin Coolidge

"If you're walking down the right path and you're willing to keep walking, eventually you'll make progress."
   Barack Obama

"The mode in which the inevitable comes to pass is through effort."
   Oliver Wendell Holmes, Jr.

"If you'll not settle for anything less than your best, you will be amazed at what you can accomplish in your lives."
   Vince Lombardi

"We don't have the right to be exhausted."
   Daniel Gordis

"Don't let anyone work harder than you do."
   Serena Williams

"I haven't failed. I've just found ten thousand ways that won't work."
   Thomas Edison

"Pain is temporary. It may last a minute, or an hour, or a day, or a year, but eventually it will subside and something else will take its place. If I quit, however, it lasts forever."
Lance Armstrong

"A drop of water hollows a stone, not by force, but by continuously dripping."
Ovid

"I am extraordinarily patient, provided I get my own way in the end."
Margaret Thatcher

"If you quit once it becomes a habit. Never quit."
Michael Jordan

POTENTIAL

"There is no heavier burden than a great potential."
Linus, in *Peanuts* by *Charles M. Schulz*

"I did the best I could with what I had."
Joe Louis

"If the lion knew his own strength, hard were it for any man to rule him."
Thomas More

"A great flame follows a little spark."
Dante

PROBLEMS

"Don't be pushed by your problems. Be led by your dreams."
Ralph Waldo Emerson

"All of the new problems are old problems forgotten."
Russian proverb

"You fix what you can fix and you let the rest go. If there ain't nothin to be done about it it aint even a problem. It's just a aggravation."
Cormac McCarthy, in *No Country for Old Men*

"It is awfully easy to be hard-boiled about everything in the daytime, but at night it is another thing."
Ernest Hemingway, in *The Sun Also Rises*

"[T]he best way out is always through."
Robert Frost

"When you are in a hole, stop digging."
Daniel Patrick Moynihan

PUNCTUALITY

"If you are there before it is over, you're on time."
Jimmy Walker

"If you are five minutes early, then you are fifteen minutes late."
Roanna Shorofsky, paraphrasing her mother, Sunny Moskowitz

"Arriving late was a way of saying that your own time was more valuable than the time of the person who waited for you."

Karen Joy Fowler

REGRET

"Maybe I did not live as I ought to have done."

Leo Tolstoy, in *The Death of Ivan Ilyich*

"Before his death, Rabbi Zusya said, 'In the coming world, they will not ask me: "Why were you not Moses?" They will ask me: "Why were you not Zusya?"'"

Martin Buber, in *Tales of the Hasidim*

"Don't let the past ruin the future."

Rachel Ringler

RETIREMENT

"I have always had a fear of continuing in office under a delusion of adequacy."

Charles Evans Hughes

"Rapid motion ought not to be succeeded by sudden rest."

John Adams

"Sooner or later I'm going to die, but I'm not going to retire."

Margaret Mead

SLEEP

"I'm not that keen on the idea of being unconscious. There's plenty of time to be unconscious coming up."
   Christopher Hitchens

"For every minute we close our eyes, we lose sixty seconds of light."
   Gabriel García Márquez

"Sleep, those little slices of death—how I loathe them."
   Edgar Allan Poe

SUCCESS

"Success is the ability to go from one failure to the next with great enthusiasm."
   Winston Churchill

"The secret of success is constancy of purpose."
   Benjamin Disraeli

"Losing is not my enemy . . . fear of losing is my enemy."
   Rafael Nadal

"No man can succeed in any calling without provoking the jealousy and envy of some. The strong level-headed man will go straight forward and do his work, and history will rightly record."
   John D. Rockefeller, Sr.

"Most successes are unhappy. That's why they are successes—they have to reassure themselves by achieving something that the world will notice."
   Agatha Christie

"Life is perverse and human beings don't get what they deserve. The people with the worst grades start the most successful businesses. The shallowest people end up blissfully happy and they are so vapid they don't even realize how vapid they are because vapidity is the only trait that comes with its own impermeable obliviousness system."

David Brooks

"As long as you view yourself as a victim, you'll never amount to anything."

Lucy Aharish

"If your success is not on your own terms, if it looks good to the world but does not feel good in your soul, it is not success at all."

Anna Quindlen

"I don't know the key to success, but the key to failure is trying to please everyone."

Bill Cosby

"Success is a lousy teacher. It seduces smart people into thinking they can't lose."

Bill Gates

"None of us got where we are solely by pulling ourselves up by our bootstraps. We got here because somebody—a parent, a teacher, an Ivy League crony or a few nuns—bent down and helped us pick up our boots."

Thurgood Marshall

"To achieve great things, two things are needed: a plan and not quite enough time."

Leonard Bernstein

"There is no disinfectant like success."
Elizabeth Taylor

"Judge your success by what you had to give up in order to get it."
Dalai Lama

TIME

"Time is of critical importance—not years or months, but seconds and split seconds. This time awareness and appreciation of it is the singular gift granted to free man, because time belongs to him: It is his time, and he can utilize it to the utmost or waste it. A free man does not want time to pass; he wants time to slow down, because to him time is a treasure."
Joseph B. Soloveitchik

"How we spend our days is, of course, how we spend our lives."
Annie Dillard

"Time stays long enough for anyone who will use it."
Leonardo da Vinci

"Dost thou love life? Then do not squander time; for that's the stuff life is made of."
Benjamin Franklin

"All we have to decide is what to do with the time that is given us."
J. R. R. Tolkien

TRAINING

"Difficult in training, easy in battle."
Alexander Suvorov

"The more you sweat in peace, the less you bleed in war."
  George S. Patton

"If you don't do it in practice, you won't do it in the game."
  Atanda Musa

YOUTH

"No one who is young is ever going to be old."
  John Steinbeck

"Youth is not a time of life but a state of mind . . . a predominance of courage over timidity, of the appetite for adventure over the love of ease."
  Robert F. Kennedy

"The young can't help acting; they're immature but they're placed in a mature world and have to act as if they were mature. So they put on whatever masks and disguises appeal to them and can be made to fit—and they act."
  Milan Kundera

"Age is foolish and forgetful when it underestimates youth."
  J. K. Rowling

"Never think of yourself as a finished product, but always as a work in progress. If you achieve that, you'll retain the sense of awe and wonder that are the underpinnings of youthfulness."
  Ted Comet

SECTION 3

Taking Charge

"Every great dream begins with a dreamer. Always remember, you have within you the strength, the patience, and the passion to reach for the stars to change the world."

Harriet Tubman

"Most people have the will to win. Few have the will to prepare to win."

Bobby Knight

ACTION

"The world is before you and you need not take it or leave it as it was when you came in."
James Baldwin

"Well done is better than well said."
Benjamin Franklin

"If you see a turtle sitting on top of a fence post, it didn't get there by accident."
Bill Clinton

"The only measure of what you believe is what you do."
Gina Rosenfeld

"Do not study as a student, but as a person who is alive and who cares. Leave the isolated world of ideological fantasy, allow your ideas to become part of your living and your living to become part of your ideas."
Tom Hayden

"Do something. If it works, do more of it. If it doesn't, do something else."
Franklin D. Roosevelt

"It is much better to make a statement with one's life than with one's mouth."
Philip Berrigan

"A single act is better than a thousand groans."
Yosef Yitzchak Schneersohn

"I would rather swim than float."
Asa Kasher

"I want to do, not just to be."
Princess Diana

"There is always something that can be done."
Richard Holbrooke

"It is not the critic who counts, not the man who points out how the strong man stumbled, or where the doer of deeds could have done better. The credit belongs to the man who is actually in the arena; whose face is marred by the dust and sweat and blood; who strives valiantly; who errs and comes short again and again; who knows the great enthusiasms, the great devotions and spends himself in a worthy cause; who at the best, knows in the end the triumph of high achievement, and who, at worst, if he fails, at least fails while daring greatly; so that his place shall never be with those cold and timid souls who know neither victory or defeat."
Theodore Roosevelt

"Whatever you do will be insignificant, but it is very important that you do it."
Mohandas Gandhi

CHOICES

"At hinge moments of history, there are never good and bad options, only bad and much worse."
Mark Steyn

"Inaction is also a decision, a policy with consequence. The wish to keep out of it all is entirely understandable, but it is every bit as much a decision as acting."
Tony Blair

"Spinach may be better for you than ice-cream, but very few people rush out to the curb when the spinach truck trundles through the neighborhood on a summer evening, tinkling its merry chimes."
Walter Russell Mead

"The choice must always be made, if not one of the lesser evil, at least of the GREATER, not the PERFECT good."
James Madison

"An excess of caution is itself a form of recklessness."
James Taranto

"In life's unforgiving arithmetic, we are the sum of our choices."
George F. Will

"Not deciding is really one of the two choices that are available."
Marilynne Robinson

DESTINY

"Nothing is inevitable."
Art Sandler

"Do not imagine that you will be able to escape in the King's palace any more than the rest of the Jews. For if you persist in keeping silent at a time like this, relief and deliverance will

come to the Jews from some other place, while you and your
father's house will perish. And who knows whether it was just
for such a time that you attained the royal position!"

   Mordechai to Esther, in *The Book of Esther*

"The greatest discovery of all time is that a person can change
his future by merely changing his attitude."

   Oprah Winfrey

"The past is the present, isn't it? It's the future, too. We all try to
lie out of that, but life won't let us."

   Eugene O'Neill

"If you were born to hang, you can't drown."

   Jamaican saying

"He can run but he can't hide."

   Joe Louis

"Demography is destiny."

   August Comte

"Cleopatra's nose: If it had been shorter, the whole face of the
earth would have changed."

   Blaise Pascal

"Everyone is in bondage to the unalterable order of things
and events . . . Only through an act of sheer heroism can one
free oneself from this order and mold a new inner experience."

   Joseph B. Soloveitchik

"Everything ends badly. It's the law of the universe."

   Rohinton Mistry

EXCELLENCE

"Don't confuse success with excellence."
Ken Burns

"Good is the enemy of great."
Jim Collins

"To regret the past, to hope in the future, and never to be satisfied with the present: that is what I spend my whole life doing."
Peter Ilyich Tchaikovsky

"Intensity is the price of excellence."
Warren Buffett

"Good intentions and hard work count for something—but in the end the only real scorecard is what were the results of all that."
John Flannery

"Perfection is not attainable. But if we chase perfection, we can catch excellence."
Vince Lombardi

"If you don't keep trying to get better, you're going to get worse."
Don Mattingly

FAME

"There's fame and there's fortune. I try to get the fortune, 'cause that's what you can spend. Fame's just an ego trip."
J. J. Cale

"Fame creates its own authority."
  Lawrence Wright

"He who seeks fame, destroys his name."
  Hillel, in *Teachings of the Fathers*

IDEALISM

"Every great dream begins with a dreamer. Always remember, you have within you the strength, the patience, and the passion to reach for the stars to change the world."
  Harriet Tubman

"Even a small light can brighten great darkness."
  Israel Baal Shem Tov

"Keep your eyes on the stars and keep your feet on the ground."
  Theodore Roosevelt

"Every form of addiction is bad, no matter whether the narcotic be alcohol, morphine or idealism."
  Carl Gustav Jung

"Idealism increases in direct proportion to one's distance from the problem."
  John Galsworthy

"The attempt to create heaven on earth is bound to create hell."
  Karl Popper

IMMORTALITY

"What, after all, is immortal fame? An empty, hollow thing. All things fade into the storied past, and in a little while are shrouded in oblivion."
Marcus Aurelius

"And on the pedestal these words appear:
'My name is Ozymandias, King of Kings:
Look upon my works, ye Mighty, and despair!'
Nothing beside remains. Round the decay
Of that colossal wreck, boundless and bare
The lone and level sands stretch far away."
Percy Bysshe Shelley, in "Ozymandias"

"Words are the only things that last forever; they are more durable than the eternal hills."
William Hazlitt

"All the people standing over Shakespeare's grave and singing his praises means a big goose egg to the Bard, and a day will come—a far-off day, but be sure it definitely is coming—when all Shakespeare's plays, for all their brilliant plots and hoity-toity iambic pentameter, and every dot of Seurat's, will be gone along with each atom in the universe."
Woody Allen

"Historically, nothing resists time, everything is transitory and perishable."
Claudio Sánchez-Albornoz

LEADERSHIP

"I'll tell you what leadership is. It's persuasion—and conciliation—and education—and patience. It's long, slow, tough work. That's the only kind of leadership I know—or believe in—or will practice."
   Dwight D. Eisenhower

"To lead the people, walk behind them."
   Lao-tzu

"A leader must walk in front of his people, but he should never go so far as to move out of their sight and hearing. That is the function of leadership."
   John Vorster

"There go the people. I must follow them, for I am their leader."
   Alexandre Ledru-Rollin

"Boys, don't be so far ahead of the parade that they don't know you're part of it."
   Alfred E. Smith

"The rule of exodus tales is that chiefs who lead in the wilderness and storm the citadels do not get to govern once their troops have occupied the city. Renegades are too combative to govern well."
   David Brooks

"Don't mistake politeness for lack of strength."
   Sonia Sotomayor

"Smart is not enough. Leadership is another thing entirely, about knowing your mind enough to make real decisions, ones that last."
   Paul A. Volcker

"Leaders are made, they are not born. They are made by hard effort, which is the price which all of us must pay to achieve any goal that is worthwhile."

Vince Lombardi

"As a general rule, the people running the world are people from blue-collar families who are lower middle class. It's rarely the case that somebody whose father was a billionaire turns out to be better than his father, becoming a multibillionaire or running the world."

David Rubenstein

"When things get tough, they send for the sons of bitches."

Ernest King, on his appointment as Navy chief after the attack on Pearl Harbor

"You don't lead by hitting people over the head—that's assault, not leadership."

Dwight D. Eisenhower

LUCK

"I'd rather be lucky than good."

Lefty Gomez

"The man who said, 'I'd rather be lucky than good,' saw deeply into life. People are afraid to face how great a part of life is dependent on luck. It's scary to think so much is out of one's control. There are moments in a match when the ball hits the top of the net and for a split second can either go forward or fall back. With a little luck, it goes forward and you win. Or maybe it doesn't and you lose."

Woody Allen, in *Match Point*

"You never know what worse luck your bad luck has saved you from."
   Cormac McCarthy

"Luck is what happens when preparation meets opportunity."
   Seneca

"Luck makes talent look like genius."
   Amity Shlaes

"You don't just luck into things as much as you'd like to think you do. You build step by step, whether it's friendships or opportunities."
   Barbara Bush

"Luck is a dividend of sweat. The more you sweat, the luckier you get."
   Ray Kroc

MEMORY

"In a long life there are thirty or thirty-five thousand days to be got through, but only a few dozen that really matter, Big Days when Something Momentous Happens. The rest—the vast majority, tens of thousands of days—are unremarkable, repetitive, even monotonous. We glide through them then instantly forget them. We tend not to think about this arithmetic when we look back on our lives. We remember the handful of Big Days and throw away the rest."
   William Landay

"Perhaps nothing is ever remembered as we first encountered it, since memory is a palimpsest on which time erases and we rewrite the same story many times."

Hillel Halkin

"Memory awakens and extinguishes at will. It dulls and sharpens actions, enlarges and shrinks those who perform them. It humbles and exalts as it desires. When summoned, it slips away, and when it returns, it will do so at the time and place that suits it. It recognizes no chief, no overseer, no classifier, no ruler. Stories mix and mingle, facts sprout new shoots. The situations and scents—oh, the scents!—encrusted there are stored in the most disorganized and wonderful manner, not chronologically, not according to size or importance or even the alphabet."

Meir Shalev

MIRACLES

"If we were to walk in the woods and a spring appeared just when we became thirsty, we would call it a miracle. And if on a second walk, if we became thirsty at just that point again the spring appeared, we would remark on the coincidence. But if that spring were always there, we would take it for granted and cease to notice it. Yet is that not more miraculous still?"

Israel Baal Shem Tov

"There are only two ways to live your life. One is as though nothing is a miracle. The other is as though everything is a miracle."

Albert Einstein

"Miracles sometimes occur. You just have to work very hard for them."

Chaim Weizmann

"Miracles are a retelling in small letters of the very same story which is written across the whole world in letters too large for some of us to see."

C. S. Lewis

OPPORTUNITY

"There is a tide in the affairs of men,
Which, taken at the flood, leads on to fortune;
Omitted, all the voyage of their life
Is bound in the shallows and in miseries . . .
And we must take the current when it serves,
Or lose our ventures."

William Shakespeare

"When one door closes another door opens; but we often look so long and so regretfully upon the closed door that we do not see the ones which open for us."

Alexander Graham Bell

"When you think of what you might lose if you do something, remember to take account of what you might lose if you don't."

Ann Althouse

"You'll always miss 100% of the shots you don't take."

Wayne Gretzky

"If you don't ask, the answer is always no."

Nora Roberts

OPTIMISM AND OPTIMISTS

"The definition of an optimist is someone who doesn't have all the facts."

Evan Bayh

"I am not opposed to optimism, but I am fearful of the kind that comes from self-delusion."

Marvin Davis

"A pessimist sees the difficulty in every opportunity; an optimist sees the opportunity in every difficulty."

Winston Churchill

"I am an optimist against my better judgment."

Abraham Joshua Heschel

PERSPECTIVE

"The mountains at a distance appear airy masses and smooth, but when beheld close, they are rough."

Pyrrho

"When you part from your friend, you grieve not; For that which you love most in him may be clearer in his absence, as the mountain to the climber is clearer from the plain."

Kahlil Gibran

"Man passes through the present with his eyes blindfolded. He is permitted merely to sense and guess at what he is actually experiencing. Only later when the cloth is untied can he glance at the

past and find out what he has experienced and what meaning it
has had."
  Milan Kundera

"Perspective aids the intellectual process, but it may distort the
event because it superimposes upon it wisdom not available at
the time."
  Louis Nizer

"We see things as we are, not as they are."
  Leo Rosten

"One must wait until the evening to see how splendid the day
has been."
  Sophocles

PLANNING

"In preparing for battle, I have always found that plans are useless but planning is indispensable."
  Dwight D. Eisenhower

"Night plans aren't any good in the morning. The way you think
at night is no good in the morning."
  Ernest Hemingway, in *For Whom the Bell Tolls*

"Everyone's got a plan until they get punched in the mouth."
  Mike Tyson

PREPARATION

"Most people have the will to win. Few have the will to prepare
to win."
  Bobby Knight

"The secret of success in life is for a man to be ready for his time when it comes."
Benjamin Disraeli

"Successful people make a habit of doing things that unsuccessful people don't like to do."
Bob Bowman

"Anticipate the difficult by managing the easy."
Lao-tzu

"If you don't know where you are going, any road will get you there."
Lewis Carroll (attributed, not confirmed)

"We are all prisoners of a rigid conception of what is important and what is not. We anxiously follow what we suppose to be important, while what we suppose to be unimportant wages guerrilla warfare behind our backs, transforming the world without our knowledge and eventually mounting a surprise attack on us."
Milan Kundera

"It's a bad time to be reading the instructions on the fire extinguisher during the fire."
John Cruden

PRINCIPLE

"If principles can become dated, they're not principles."
Warren Buffett

"Consensus seems to be the process of abandoning all beliefs, principles, values and policies in search of something in which no one believes, but to which no one objects—the process of avoiding the very issues that have to be solved, merely because you cannot get agreement on the way ahead. What great cause would have been fought and won under the banner 'I stand for consensus'?"

Margaret Thatcher

"It is often easier to fight for a principle than to live up to it."

Adlai Stevenson

REMEMBRANCE

"To forgive and forget is easier than to remember."

Reuben Ainsztein

"Memories fade when not re-lived, and they are not re-lived if they are only painful. Memories filled with stories of love, courage, survival, passion, and religious depth, however, sustain the growing spirit of people of all ages."

Dov Lerea

"History is amoral: events occurred. But memory is moral; what we consciously remember is what our conscience remembers. . . . History and memory share events; that is, they share time and space. Every moment is two moments."

Anne Michaels

REPUTATION

"Flies in a restaurant on a single day in summer may drive patrons elsewhere, never to return."

Woodford Patterson

"You can't build a reputation on what you're going to do."
Henry Ford

"Let us endeavor so to live that when we come to die even the undertaker will be sorry."
Mark Twain

"When tempted to do anything in secret, ask yourself if you would do it in public. If you would not, be sure it is wrong."
Thomas Jefferson

"A public image, once registered, is almost impossible to re-photograph: later exposures only darken the underlying silhouette."
Edmund Morris

"Once smeared, always vulnerable."
Woody Allen

"The shadows cast by great men change shape over time depending on the angle of illumination, diminishing in harsh overhead light or expanding in the glow of distant perspective."
Edward Rothstein

"There is no one you cannot make out to be in some way odd, or a figure of ridicule, if you pry and probe into their life with sufficient ruthlessness."
Tony Blair

"A great name is more powerful than riches."
Miguel de Cervantes

"Nothing deflates so fast as a punctured reputation."
Thomas Dewar

"Even if no salvation should come, I want to be worthy of it at every moment."
    Franz Kafka

"It takes two decades to build a reputation and five minutes to ruin it."
    Warren Buffett

RESPONSIBILITY

"There's no such thing as a free lunch."
    Walter Morrow

"If someone has to eat meat, someone has to do the slaughtering."
    Isaac Bashevis Singer

"Conduct yourself as if the fate of your nation depends on your actions and the responsibility was yours alone."
    Johann Gottlieb Fichte

"In a free society, some are guilty, but all are responsible."
    Abraham Joshua Heschel

"Do you feel shame because you are alive in place of someone else? A person more generous, sensitive, wise, useful and worthy of living than you? You cannot exclude the possibility. It's just a supposition that each is a Cain to his brother, that each of us has betrayed his neighbor and is living in his place. It's a supposition, but it gnaws at you; it's nesting deep inside like a worm. It gnaws, and it shrieks."
    Primo Levi

"The fault, dear Brutus, is not in our stars, But in ourselves."
William Shakespeare

"You are not obliged to finish the task, neither are you free to neglect it."
Tarfon, in *Teachings of the Fathers*

RISK

"We all assume certain risks in whatever we do, whatever activities we pursue, and regardless of how experienced, careful and dedicated we are. Accidents do and will happen."
Harry M. Whittington

"Nothing in life is so exhilarating as to be shot at without result."
Winston Churchill

"Life is best organized as a series of daring ventures from a secure base."
John Bowlby

TRUST

"Better to be occasionally cheated than perpetually suspicious."
Bertie Charles Forbes

"The greatest trick the Devil ever pulled was convincing the world he didn't exist."
Christopher McQuarrie, in *The Usual Suspects*

"People who want to be deluded are going to be deluded no matter what they are told."
John F. Kennedy

"Whoever is careless with the truth in small matters cannot be trusted with important matters."
Albert Einstein

"The less prudence with which others conduct their affairs, the greater the prudence with which we should conduct our own affairs."
Warren Buffett

"The louder he talked of his honor, the faster we counted our spoons."
Ralph Waldo Emerson

"Don't ever take a fence down until you know why it was put up."
Robert Frost

"Trust is the glue of life."
Stephen R. Covey

Love, Family, and Friends

"Friends bear witness to who we really are. They have no bond of blood, or marriage vows, no contracts, or documentation. Friends are voluntary, and they reflect the best qualities we nourish in our inner selves."
  Stanley E. Flink

"Parenting is no sport for perfectionists."
  Andrew Solomon

CHILDHOOD AND CHILDREARING

"First, a milkshake and a nap, and then we'll talk."
  Rachel Ringler

"The letters received from parents are messages sent from a stronghold from which one is continually receding, and serve only to make you conscious of your alienation."
  Milan Kundera

"I want to give my children enough that they can do anything, but not so much that they can do nothing."
  Warren Buffett

"Your children are not your children. . . . They come through you, but not from you."
  Kahlil Gibran

"When sons are unhappy, they remember their mothers."
  Rohinton Mistry

"When a child first catches adults out—when it first walks into his grave little head that adults do not always have divine intelligence, that their judgments are not always wise, their thinking true, their sentences just—his world falls into panic desolation. The gods are fallen and all safety gone. And there is one sure thing about the fall of gods; they do not fall a little; they crash and shatter or sink deeply into green muck . . . And the child's world is never quite whole again."
  John Steinbeck

"Children learn more from what you are than what you teach."
W. E. B. Du Bois

"Parents are programmed to want the best for their kids, re-gardless of what they get in return. That's what love is supposed to be like, right? But in fact, if you think about it, that's kind of a strange belief. Given what we know about the way people really are. Selfish and shortsighted and egotistical and needy. Why should being a parent, just in and of itself, somehow con-fer superior-personhood on everybody who tries it?"
Jonathan Franzen

"Accustom your children constantly to this; if a thing happened at one window, and they, when relating it, say that it happened at another, do not let it pass, but instantly check them; you do not know where deviation from truth will end."
Samuel Johnson

"A child becomes an adult when he realizes that he has a right not only to be right but also to be wrong."
Thomas Szasz

"Train up a child in the way he should go and even when he is old he shall not depart from it."
Proverbs 22:6

"Parenting is no sport for perfectionists."
Andrew Solomon

"Give the ones you love wings to fly, roots to come back, and reasons to stay."
Dalai Lama

DEATH

"Death ends a life, but it does not end a relationship, which struggles on in the survivor's mind towards some resolution which it may never find."
Robert Anderson

"If you focus on mortality, the house always wins."
Woody Allen

"It helps to die early if you want a big funeral."
Jonathan Franzen

"Life is tragic simply because the earth turns and the sun inexorably rises and sets, and one day, for each of us, the sun will go down for the last, last time."
James Baldwin

"I can't die but once."
Harriet Tubman

DINING

"As a child, my family's menu consisted of two choices: take it or leave it."
Buddy Hackett

"Never underestimate the importance of a good meal. It brings people together and can also draw them close."
Rachel Ringler

"After a good dinner, one can forgive anybody, even one's own relatives."
Oscar Wilde

"A party without cake is just a meeting."
Julia Child

FAMILY

"What can you do to promote world peace? Go home and love your family."
Mother Teresa

"At the end of your life you will never regret not having passed one more test, not winning one more verdict, or not closing one more deal. You will regret time not spent with a husband, a friend, a child or a parent."
Barbara Bush

"A happy family is but an earlier heaven."
George Bernard Shaw

"All happy families are alike; each unhappy family is unhappy in its own way."
Leo Tolstoy

"The family is one of Nature's masterpieces."
George Santayana

"A dysfunctional family is any family with more than one person in it."
Mary Karr

"When you start talking about family, about lineage and ancestry, you are talking about every person on earth."
   Alex Haley

"There is nothing like unexpected good fortune to make a family miserable."
   Randy Cohen

FORGIVENESS

"When a person forgives, it is as if he were saying to the forgiven: I am willing to bear this burden with you. From now on, it will be shared by both of us, and we will struggle with it together. The forgiver embraces the forgiven. The burden does not disappear. It is not forgotten. Instead, it becomes their joint legacy."
   Yotam Benziman

"There are two conditions for forgiveness: The good will of the offended party and the full awareness of the offender."
   Emmanuel Levinas

"Even if an act could be forgiven, no one could bear the responsibility of forgiveness on behalf of the dead. No act of violence is ever resolved. When the one who can forgive can no longer speak, there is only silence."
   Anne Michaels

FRIENDSHIP

"Friends bear witness to who we really are. They have no bond of blood, or marriage vows, no contracts, or documentation.

Friends are voluntary, and they reflect the best qualities we nourish in our inner selves."

Stanley E. Flink

"I have no love for a friend who loves in words alone."

Sophocles

"Friendship, of itself a holy tie, is made more sacred by adversity."

John Dryden

"He was surrounded with a circle of acquaintances; he called them friends for short."

August Strindberg

"The holy passion of Friendship is of so sweet and steady and loyal and enduring a nature that it will last through a whole lifetime, if not asked to lend money."

Mark Twain

"Anyone can sympathize with the sufferings of a friend, but it requires a very fine nature to sympathize with a friend's success."

Oscar Wilde

"Life is a process in which you collect people and prune them when they stop working for you."

Taffy Brodesser-Akner

"A friend in power is a friend lost."

Henry Adams

"Our perfect companions never have fewer than four feet."

Sidonie-Gabrielle Colette

GOSSIP

"Gossip hurts all three parties: the gossiper, the one who receives the gossip, and the one gossiped about."
   Isaac Bashevis Singer

"If someone says your sister is a prostitute, it will take you ten years to prove that you don't have a sister."
   Israeli saying

"Don't pay any attention to what they write about you. Just measure it in inches."
   Andy Warhol

"If you haven't got anything good to say about anyone, come and sit by me."
   Alice Roosevelt Longworth

"There is only one thing in the world worse than being talked about, and that is not being talked about."
   Oscar Wilde

GRATITUDE

"Someone's sitting in the shade today because someone planted a tree a long time ago."
   Warren Buffett

"Even if a person borrows money from another and then repays it, he still owes gratitude. He has discharged the money debt but the obligation remains."
   Benjamin Franklin

"We sleep soundly in our beds because rough men stand ready in the night to visit violence on those who would do us harm."
  George Orwell

"The good you do today, people will often forget tomorrow. Do good anyway."
  Mother Teresa

HEROES

"Only in epic poems are heroes humanly attractive. More usually in real life their dedication makes them unrelenting; their courage makes them overbearing; they are out of scale and therefore not amenable to ordinary mortal intercourse."
  Henry A. Kissinger

"Every hero becomes a bore at last."
  Ralph Waldo Emerson

"Show me a hero, and I will write you a tragedy."
  F. Scott Fitzgerald

"The public always tires of its messiahs, and sooner or later invariably turns them out, whether they be good, which is uncommon, or bad, which is the rule."
  H. L. Mencken

"Fans always need to feel uniquely connected to the object of their fandom; they jealously guard those points of connection, however tiny or imaginary, that justify the feeling of uniqueness."
  Jonathan Franzen

"Resilience, inventiveness, and survivorship—qualities often ascribed to great physicians—are reflected qualities, emanating first from those who struggle with illness and only then mirrored by those who treat them. If the history of medicine is told through the stories of doctors, it is because their contributions stand in place of the more substantive heroism of their patients."
Siddhartha Mukherjee

"We can't all be heroes. Some of us have to stand on the curb and clap as they go by."
Will Rogers

INDISPENSABILITY

"There are times when the fate of an entire people rests on a handful of fighters and volunteers. They must secure the uprightness of our world in one short hour. In such moments, they have no one to ask, no one to turn to. The commanders on the spot determine the fate of the battle."
Shimon Peres

"There is no nation which has not, at one period or another, experienced an absolute necessity of the services of particular men in particular situations; perhaps it would not be too strong to say, to the preservation of its political existence."
Alexander Hamilton

"Enlightened statesmen will not always be at the helm."
James Madison

"Graveyards are full of indispensable men."
Charles de Gaulle

JEALOUSY

"In jealousy, a feeling is a reason."
  Howard Jacobson

"We must believe in luck. For how else can we explain the success of those we don't like?"
  Jean Cocteau

"Moral indignation is jealousy with a halo."
  H. G. Wells

"Never speak disrespectfully of high society. Only people who can't get into it do that."
  Oscar Wilde

"Everybody pities the weak; jealousy you have to earn."
  Arnold Schwarzenegger

LOVE AND ROMANCE

"Anyone who loves intensely lives not in himself but in the object of his love, and the further he can move out of himself into his love, the happier he is."
  Desiderius Erasmus

"The most painful thing is losing yourself in the process of loving someone too much, and forgetting that you are special too."
  Ernest Hemingway

"The very essence of romance is uncertainty."
  Oscar Wilde

"Every love relationship is based on unwritten conventions rashly agreed upon by the lovers during the first weeks of their love . . . O lovers! Be wary during those perilous first days! If you serve the other party breakfast in bed, you will be obliged to continue same in perpetuity or face charges of animosity and treason!"

Milan Kundera

"A broken heart sometimes stretches when it mends."

Herman Wouk

"As a face opposite water reflects another face, so do people reflect each other's hearts."

Proverbs 27:19

"Listening is an act of love."

Dave Isay

"A bed takes up a very small space in a house. You don't spend a marriage sleeping with a person but waking with her."

Herman Wouk

"When love is strong, a man and a woman can make their bed on a sword's blade; when love is weak, a bed of sixty cubits is not large enough."

Talmud: Sanhedrin

"A successful marriage requires falling in love many times, always with the same person."

Mignon McLaughlin

"Young love is about wanting to be happy. Old love is about wanting someone else to be happy."

Mary Pipher

RELATIONSHIPS

"People will forget what you said, people will forget what you did, but people will never forget how you made them feel."
   Maya Angelou

"When we get partial information about others, we tend to fill in the gaps optimistically; we assume that they are wonderful, just like us, and that they share our exact values and preferences."
   Dan Ariely

"What we know of other people is only our memory of the moments during which we knew them. And they have changed since then."
   T. S. Eliot

"Dependency breeds hostility."
   Richard Ekstract

"The other side of interference is support."
   Francesca Segal

"Sometimes, you just don't like somebody."
   Henry Ford II, on firing Lee Iacocca

"Indifference and neglect often do much more damage than outright dislike."
   J. K. Rowling

"Lots of people want to ride with you in the limo, but what you want is someone who will take the bus with you when the limo breaks down."
   Oprah Winfrey

"Iron sharpens iron, and one person sharpens another."
Proverbs 27:17

"A smile is the shortest distance between two people."
Victor Borge

REUNIONS

"Every time I have ever stepped back into the life of someone I used to know but have not seen for ten or fifteen or twenty years, the results have been the same: embarrassment, a lack of things to say, and mutual disappointment over the evidence that time has not stood still for either of us. Paths that run together for a time, and then diverge for a substantial period, rarely come together smoothly again."
Jerome Tuccille

"You're many years late,
How happy I am to see you."
Anna Akhmatova

SECRETS

"There are secrets that the heart cannot reveal to the lips."
Isaac Bashevis Singer

"After a time, having a secret and nobody knowing you have a secret is no fun. And although you don't want others to know what the secret is, you want them to at least know you have one."
E. L. Konigsburg

"There is no privacy."
Warren Beatty

SELF-INTEREST

"By pursuing his own interest, the individual frequently promotes that of the society more effectually than when he really intends to promote it. I have never known much good done by those who affected to trade for the public good."

Adam Smith

"I stick my neck out for nobody. I'm the only cause I'm interested in."

Humphrey Bogart, in *Casablanca* by *Julius* and *Philip Epstein* and *Howard Koch*

"My paper cut concerns me more than your cancer."

Benjamin Siegel

SEX

"I don't know if it's good and I don't know if it's bad. All I know is that there is nothing quite like it."

W. C. Fields

"Procreation is nature's principal occupation, and every man, whether he be young or old, when meeting any woman, measures the potentiality of sex between them."

Charlie Chaplin

"Sex is a perverse little devil and the minute you ignore it, it has a serious temper tantrum and tries every trick in the book to get you to notice it. It clamors for your attention until it gets it, at which point it disappears."

Cynthia Heimel

"Forbidden fruit has its brown spots, but these are not seen in the dusky glow of appetite; one has to bite and taste the unpleasant mush."

Herman Wouk

"Lord, make me chaste, but not yet."

Augustine

Creativity and Ideas

"If you have an apple and I have an apple and we exchange these apples then you and I will still each have one apple. But if you have an idea and I have an idea and we exchange these ideas, then each of us will have two ideas."
George Bernard Shaw

"Stronger than any army is an idea whose time has come."
Victor Hugo

CHANGE

"You cannot step into the same river twice."
Heraclitus

"Isn't it funny how day by day nothing changes, but when you look back everything is different?"
C. S. Lewis

"It takes only one generation for things to feel authentic. Because what feels authentic is what we grow up with."
Lori Lefkovitz

"Stability is a surface illusion, like a frozen river; underneath, the currents are moving, and to the casual observer the ice looks equally stable whether there's a foot of it or just two inches. There is no status quo. . . . Stability is a fancy term to dignify inertia and complacency as sophistication."
Mark Steyn

"No man can struggle with advantage against the spirit of his age and country, and however powerful a man may be, it is hard for him to make his contemporaries share feelings and ideas which run counter to the general run of their hopes and desires."
Alexis de Tocqueville

"All rivers run to the sea and yet the sea is not full, and from the place where they began, there they return again."
Ecclesiastes

"If we want things to stay as they are, then things will have to change."

Giuseppe Tomasi di Lampedusa

CREATIVITY

"Creativity is just connecting things. When you ask creative people how they did something, they feel a little guilty because they didn't really do it, they just saw something. It seemed obvious to them after a while."

Steve Jobs

"If you're not prepared to be wrong, you'll never come up with anything original."

Ken Robinson

"Invent first and then embellish."

Samuel Johnson

"If you make up some kind of a formula, you are giving up."

Isaac Mizrahi

"Millions saw the apple fall, Newton was the only one who asked why?"

Bernard M. Baruch

DESIGN

"Design is not just what it looks like and feels like. Design is how it works."

Steve Jobs

"An interesting plainness is the most difficult and precious thing to achieve."

Ludwig Mies van der Rohe

"To be truly elegant, one should not be noticed."

Beau Brummell

"While great art makes you wonder, great design makes things clear."

John Maeda

DISSENT

"To speak no evil, of evil, is evil."

Niccolo Machiavelli

"Public silence is not neutral. It supports the policy status quo. If the policy turns out to be disastrous, those who swallowed their concerns about it—who by their public silence gave the appearance of accepting it—will surely not be free of responsibility."

Anthony Lewis

"The men who create power make an indispensable contribution to the nation's greatness, but the men who question power make a contribution just as indispensable, especially when that questioning is disinterested, for they determine whether we use power or power uses us."

John F. Kennedy

"Since when have we Americans been expected to bow submissively to authority and speak with awe and reverence to those who represent us? The constitutional theory is that we the people are the sovereigns, the state and federal officials only our agents. We who have the final word can speak softly or angrily. We can seek to challenge and annoy, as we need not stay docile and quiet."

William O. Douglas

"Freedom to differ is not limited to things that do not matter much. That would be a mere shadow of freedom. The test of its substance is the right to differ as to things that touch the heart of the existing order."

Robert H. Jackson

"A long habit of not thinking a thing wrong gives it a superficial appearance of being right, and raises at first a formidable outcry in defense of custom."

Thomas Paine

FACTS

"Everyone is entitled to their own opinions, but they are not entitled to their own facts."

Daniel Patrick Moynihan

"The plural of anecdote isn't data."

George Stigler

"There are knowns, known unknowns, and unknown unknowns. The unknown unknowns, we don't even know we don't know them."

Donald Rumsfeld

FREEDOM OF SPEECH

"Freedom of speech includes the freedom not to speak."
   Milton R. Konvitz

"If liberty means anything, it means the right to tell people what they do not want to hear."
   George Orwell

"Democracy depends on the idea that we hold each other's right to express ourselves and be heard above our own desire to always get the outcomes we want."
   Mark Zuckerberg

"We can never allow people who use non-democratic means, people who use violence instead of arguments, people who use knives instead of debates, we can never allow them to set the agenda."
   Geert Wilders

"I believe in freedom of speech, but I also believe that we have an obligation to condemn speech that is racist, bigoted, anti-Semitic, or hateful."
   John R. Lewis

"We don't silence, jail or kill people with whom we disagree just because their ideas are offensive or disturbing. We believe that when such ideas are openly debated, they sink of their own weight and attract few followers."
   Peter Hoekstra

"Being shocked is part of democratic debate. Being shot is not."
   Dominique Sopo

"Censorship, like slavery, can never be legal, even if embodied a thousand times in laws and regulations."
   Karl Marx

"There is a thought that stops thought. That is the only thought that ought to be stopped."
   G. K. Chesterton

"Why bother winning the debate when it's easier to close it down?"
   Mark Steyn

"If we extend unlimited tolerance even to those who are intolerant, if we are not prepared to defend a tolerant society against the onslaught of the intolerant, then the tolerant will be destroyed, and tolerance with them."
   Karl Popper

"The right to be heard does not automatically include the right to be taken seriously."
   Hubert H. Humphrey

"If you don't support free speech for people who you disagree with, then you don't support free speech."
   Ricky Gervais

FUTURE

"People are always shouting they want to create a better future. It's not true. The future is an apathetic void of no interest to anyone. The past is full of life, eager to irritate us, provoke and insult us, tempt us to destroy or repaint it. The only reason

people want to be masters of the future is to change the past. They are fighting for access to the laboratories where photographs are retouched and biographies and histories rewritten."
Milan Kundera

"Ah, 'the future'—that seductively fabricated illusion, fraudulently framed as the promise of serene tranquility, tantalizingly close at hand, and conveniently decoupled from the trauma and tragedy of the past."
Martin Sherman

"Life can only be understood backwards; but it must be lived forwards."
Søren Kierkegaard

"It is difficult to make predictions, especially about the future."
Sam Goldwyn

"The best way to predict your future is to create it."
Abraham Lincoln

GENIUS

"Genius is finding the invisible link between things."
Vladimir Nabokov

"Genius, no matter how rare, is a human universal. It sends into the world new perception and new experience, inspiring duplication: Out of Israel came monotheism, out of Greece philosophy, out of Arab civilization science and poetry, out of England the Magna Carta, out of France the Enlightenment."
Cynthia Ozick

"Able methodical people grow on every bush but genius comes once in a generation and if you ever get in its vicinity thank the Lord—and stick."

Ida Tarbell

HISTORY

"History is lived forward, but it is written in retrospect. We know the end before we consider the beginning and we can never wholly recapture what it was to know the beginning only."

C. V. Wedgwood

"Turned wrong way round, the relentless unforeseen was what we schoolchildren studied as 'History,' harmless history, where everything unexpected in its own time is chronicled on the page as inevitable. The terror of the unforeseen is what the science of history hides, turning a disaster into an epic."

Philip Roth

"By the very nature of his task, the historian is like the mystery fan who reads the last chapter first."

Scott D. Sagan

"What experience and history teach is this: That people and governments never have learned anything from history."

Georg Wilhelm Friedrich Hegel

"The doors of history swing on tiny hinges. Nothing is more barren and futile than speculation on what might have been."

John L. Lewis

"History is the poisoned well, seeping into the groundwater. It's not the unknown past we're doomed to repeat, but the past we know. Every recorded event is a brick of potential, of precedent, thrown into the future. Eventually the idea will hit someone in the back of the head. This is the duplicity of history: an idea recorded will become an idea resurrected. Out of fertile ground, the compost of history."

Anne Michaels

"History is a set of lies agreed upon."

Napoleon

"History is not what's done. It's what gets into writing."

Meir Shalev

"History is that certainty produced at the point where the imperfections of memory meet the inadequacies of documentation."

Julian Barnes

"History is not interesting—what is interesting is the anecdote."

Karl Lagerfeld

IDEAS

"If you have an apple and I have an apple and we exchange these apples then you and I will still each have one apple. But if you have an idea and I have an idea and we exchange these ideas, then each of us will have two ideas."

George Bernard Shaw

"Every new idea is first ridiculed, then vigorously attacked, and, finally, taken for granted."

Arthur Schopenhauer

"No man is wealthy or powerful enough to move a nation. Only an idea can achieve that."
   Theodor Herzl

"The empires of the future are the empires of the mind."
   Winston Churchill

"In philosophy, or religion, or ethics, or politics, two and two might make five, but when one was designing a gun or an airplane they had to make four. Inefficient nations were always conquered sooner or later."
   George Orwell

"The field of knowledge is the common property of all mankind."
   Thomas Jefferson

"Power comes not from knowledge kept but from knowledge shared."
   Bill Gates

"Minds fill the pockets. Pockets don't fill the mind."
   Shimon Peres

"I've always comforted myself with the notion that the best ideas win out. But ideas cannot win on their own. They need a voice. They need a hearing. Above all, they must be backed by people willing to live by them."
   Bari Weiss

"To doubt everything or to believe everything are two equally convenient solutions. Both dispense with the need for thought."
   Henri Poincaré

"Controversial proposals, once accepted, soon become hallowed."
Dean Acheson

"Stronger than any army is an idea whose time has come."
Victor Hugo

IDEOLOGY

"A historical hallmark of 'isms' and charismatic movements is to dig deeper when they falter—to insist that the 'thing' itself, whether it be Peronism, or socialism, etc., had not been tried but that the leader had been undone by forces that hemmed him in."
Fouad Ajami

"The same words that carry a good many people into the howling wilderness in one generation are irksome or meaningless in the next."
Marilynne Robinson

"No great movement designed to change the world can bear to be laughed at or belittled, because laughter is a rust corroding everything."
Milan Kundera

"No matter if it is a white cat or a black cat. As long as it can catch mice, it is a good cat."
Deng Xiaoping

NORMS

"Once the standard is set, the unacceptable gains respectability, and the sentiments are no longer out of bounds."
Jennifer Rubin

"Nothing is normal—it is purely a statistical construct. Actually, not normal is more normal."
   Felicia Marcus

PACIFISM

"It is useless for the sheep to pass resolutions in favor of vegetarianism while the wolf remains of a different opinion."
   William Ralph Inge

"Sometimes you have to pick the gun up to put the Gun down."
   Malcolm X

"Pacifist propaganda can only be effective against those countries where a certain amount of freedom of speech is still permitted; in other words it is helpful to totalitarianism. . . . Despotic governments can stand 'moral force' till the cows come home; what they fear is physical force."
   George Orwell

"Sometimes, a war saves people."
   José Ramos-Horta

PERSUASION

"Points don't stay proven and battles don't stay won."
   George F. Will

"The most difficult subjects can be explained to the most slow-witted man if he has not formed any idea of them already; but the simplest thing cannot be made clear to the most intelligent

man if he is firmly persuaded that he knows already, without a shadow of a doubt, what is laid before him."
Leo Tolstoy

"If you can get people to see the world as you do, you have unwittingly framed every subsequent choice."
David Brooks

"If you would win a man to your cause, first convince him that you are his sincere friend."
Abraham Lincoln

"No one has ever been insulted into agreement."
Arthur C. Brooks

"Charm is a way of getting the answer 'Yes' without having asked any clear question."
Albert Camus

"First, you win the argument, then you win the vote."
Margaret Thatcher

"You can't turn a 'no' into a 'yes' without a 'maybe' in between."
Frank Pugliese

POLITICAL SPEECH AND SPEECHES

"Political language is designed to make lies sound truthful and murder respectable, and to give an appearance of solidity to pure wind."
George Orwell, in "Politics and the English Language"

"Speeches aren't magic. A speech is only as good as the ideas it advances."

Peggy Noonan

"Communication is fifty percent of the battle in the information age. Say it once, say it twice and keep saying it, and when you've finished, you'll know you still haven't said it enough."

Bill Clinton

"Political speeches often contain long passages that are put there to sound nice rather than to convey any serious meaning or thought."

Walter Russell Mead

"A campaign speech is a poster, not an etching."

Michael Kramer

"In politics, a failure of communication is always the fault of the communicator."

Bret Stephens

"Banning political ads favors incumbents and whoever the media covers."

Mark Zuckerberg

"The whole art of a political speech is to put nothing into it. It is much more difficult than it sounds."

Hilaire Belloc

QUOTATIONS

"The whole point of a perfect quotation is to use it as quickly and as often as possible, before the rest of them, whoever they are, catch on and find out and steal it for themselves."

John Leonard

"Most of us cannot afford a spokesman. But we can all afford a quotation, which gives us many of the same advantages. Then we can deny that we said it, or if we prefer we can claim credit for choosing so graceful a way of saying it."
Daniel Boorstin

"Famous quotations become famous because, for many people, they have an irresistible allure. Yet their wording, their meaning, and, particularly, their origins have often been fictionalized by the popular mind or by careless quoters or people with an axe to grind."
Fred R. Shapiro

"Whoever repeats a word in the name of the person who said it brings redemption to the world."
Teachings of the Fathers

"We hoard quotations like amulets. They are charms against chaos, secret mantras for dark times, strings that vibrate forever in defiance of the laws of time and space. That they may be opaque or banal to everyone else is what makes them precious: they aren't supposed to work for everybody. They're there to work for us."
Louis Menand

"He'd either have to improve his memory or else never think about quotations, because when you missed one, it hung in your mind like a name you had forgotten and you could not get rid of it."
Ernest Hemingway, in *For Whom the Bell Tolls*

"He that tries to recommend [Shakespeare] by select quotations, will succeed like the pedant in Hierocles, who, when he offered his house to sale, carried a brick in his pocket as a specimen."
Samuel Johnson

"By necessity, by proclivity, and by delight, we all quote."
   Ralph Waldo Emerson

"When one begins to live by habit and by quotation, one has begun to stop living."
   James Baldwin

TRAVEL

"A good traveler has no fixed plans and is not intent on arriving."
   Lao-tzu

"Anybody who travels knows that you aren't traveling to move around. You are traveling in order to be moved. Really, what you are seeing isn't just the Grand Canyon or the Great Wall, but some moods or intimations or places inside yourself that you never ordinarily see when you are sleepwalking through your daily life."
   Pico Iyer

"The traveler sees what he sees. The tourist sees what he has come to see."
   G. K. Chesterton

"Though we travel the world over to find the beautiful, we must carry it with us, or we find it not."
   Ralph Waldo Emerson

"I have found out that there ain't no surer way to find out whether you like people or hate them than to travel with them."
   Mark Twain

WISDOM

"And I gave my heart to know wisdom, and to know madness and folly: I perceived that this also is vexation of spirit. For in much wisdom is much grief: and he that increaseth knowledge increaseth sorrow."

Ecclesiastes

"Where ignorance is bliss, 'tis folly to be wise."

Thomas Gray, from *On a Distant Prospect of Eton College*

"We may be inspired, comforted, amused or educated by quotes, and if the quote is put into the mouth of a celebrated sage, so much the better. We impress ourselves or others with the borrowed wisdom of the sage."

Fred R. Shapiro

"Wisdom too often never comes, and so one ought not to reject it merely because it comes late."

Felix Frankfurter

WORDS

"Any word one uses from habit means nothing at all."

Graham Greene

"Few ideas are correct ones, and none can ascertain which they are. But it is with words we govern men."

Benjamin Disraeli

"Euphemisms inevitably lose their soothing power as they come to be understood as the actual name for that to which they refer."

James Taranto

"The difference between the right word and the almost right word is the difference between lightning and the lightning bug."

Mark Twain

SECTION 6

Arts and Entertainment

"The artist faces a constant sense of defeat. You're working, you're trying, but it's never as good as you wanted, as you dreamed. Even your most successful work only comes close."

Peggy Noonan

"You don't make a photograph just with a camera. You bring to the act of photography all the pictures you have seen, the books you have read, the music you have heard, the people you have loved."

Ansel Adams

ART AND ARTISTS

"The persuasiveness of a true work of art is completely irrefutable; it prevails even over a resisting heart."
  Alexander Solzhenitsyn, in his Nobel Prize lecture

"The artist brings something into the world that didn't exist before, and he does it without destroying something else. A kind of refutation of the conservation of matter."
  John Updike

"The artist's function is to transfigure his experience, not to revel in it."
  Amos Elon

"All art is egocentric. Beethoven assumes that you want to listen to those goddamn symphonies of his."
  Ned Rorem

"One of the ridiculous aspects of being a poet is the huge gulf between how seriously we take ourselves and how generally we are ignored by everybody else."
  Billy Collins

"Art anchored in politics is almost always art condemned to early demise."
  Joseph Epstein

"Amateurs sit and wait for inspiration. The rest of us just get up and go to work."

Stephen King

"If you're succeeding too much, you're doing something wrong. Some artists don't have that value. They find something they can do superbly, and they love doing it, and they keep on doing it, and the audiences grow to depend on it. I think that's a mistake."

Woody Allen

"The artist faces a constant sense of defeat. You're working, you're trying, but it's never as good as you wanted, as you dreamed. Even your most successful work only comes close."

Peggy Noonan

"The world population of artists has exploded, almost no one is not an artist now."

Nicole Krauss

BIOGRAPHY AND AUTOBIOGRAPHY

"No man's life can be encompassed in one telling. There is no way to give each year its allotted weight, to include each event, each person who helped to shape a lifetime. What can be done is to be faithful in spirit to the record and try to find one's way to the heart of the man."

John Briley

"The most glorious exploits do not always furnish us with the clearest discoveries of virtue or vice in men. Sometimes a matter of less moment—an expression or a jest—informs us better of their characters and inclinations."

Plutarch

"Historians need to treat a participant's own explanation of events with a certain skepticism. It is often the statement made with an eye to the future that is most suspect."

Julian Barnes

"The autobiographer, if he be not a literary man, first hesitates through sheer cowardice—I know I did. He no sooner dips his pen than the thought at once rushes upon him that book-making is a trade like every other, and he is aghast at his own vanity which made him think for a moment that he could accomplish a task which men of learning, taste and experience would hesitate to undertake."

Joseph Jefferson, in *The Autobiography of Joseph Jefferson*

"Never trust biographies. Too many events in a man's life are invisible. Unknown to others as our dreams."

Anne Michaels

BOOKS AND LITERATURE

"There is no frigate like a book to take us lands away."

Emily Dickinson

"Make thy books thy companions. Let thy cases and shelves be thy pleasure grounds and gardens."

Judah ibn Tibbon

"I think we ought to read only the kind of books that wound and stab us. We need the books that affect us like a disaster, that grieve us deeply, like the death of someone we loved more than ourselves, like being banished into forests far from everyone, like a suicide. A book must be the ax for the frozen sea inside us."

Franz Kafka

"There is no excuse for tedious literature that does not intrigue the reader, uplift his spirit, give him joy and the escape that true art always grants."
  Isaac Bashevis Singer, in his Nobel Prize lecture

"If you want a new idea, open an old book."
  Zion Suleiman

"Hold a book in your hand and you're a pilgrim at the gates of a new city."
  Anne Michaels

"I was made for the library, not the classroom."
  Ta-Nehisi Coates

"If you write a hundred articles, all that remains of them is the distorted interpretation imposed by your adversaries. A book may not avoid every possible misinterpretation, but at least it makes certain kinds of misunderstandings impossible."
  Albert Camus

"Where books are burnt, human beings are destined to be burnt, too."
  Heinrich Heine

"The books that the world calls immoral are the books that show the world its own shame."
  Oscar Wilde

"Reading brings us unknown friends."
  Honoré de Balzac

"If you don't like to read, you haven't found the right book."
  J. K. Rowling

CUISINE

"Tell me what you eat and I will tell you what you are."
Jean Anthelme Brillat-Savarin

"The only real stumbling block is fear of failure. In cooking you've got to have a 'what-the-hell' attitude."
Julia Child

"Restaurant food is not normally harmonic. It tends to be discordant (sweet and sour, soft and hard, fruit and savory) and intensified, more salt than you use at home, more pepper; it has texture, contrast, crackle. Probably because, in a restaurant, food is a business transaction: it wants you to notice what you have paid for."
Bill Buford

"Knowledge is knowing that a tomato is a fruit. Wisdom is not putting it in a fruit salad."
Miles Kington

"The only way to preserve a cuisine is to cook it."
Janna Gur

"One of the secrets, and pleasures, of cooking is to learn to correct something if it goes awry; and one of the lessons is to grin and bear it if it cannot be fixed."
Julia Child

"Life is a combination of magic and pasta."
Federico Fellini

ENTERTAINMENT

"Hollywood is the only place where you can die of encouragement."
Pauline Kael

"Formulas are truly the backbone of the comic strip. In fact, they are probably the backbone of any continuing entertainment."
Charles M. Schulz

"With their simple and unequivocal rules, games are like so many islands of order in the vague, untidy chaos of life."
Aldous Huxley

"The only 'ism' Hollywood believes in is plagiarism."
Dorothy Parker

HUMOR AND COMEDY

"Humor is the sudden disruption of thought, the conjoining of unlikely elements."
S. J. Perelman

"Humor is based on surprise, on the violation of expectations."
Terrence Rafferty

"Tragedy is when I cut my finger. Comedy is when you walk into an open sewer and die."
Mel Brooks

"An old joke is a new joke if you haven't heard it before."
Joe Smith

"An actor playing comedy must take his role with the utmost seriousness, or else he runs the risk of amusing his audience with his performance instead of with his role."
Christopher Lehmann-Haupt

"Comedy needs fools with funny faces, but comedy without gentleness is often just sadism. It isn't that sadism can't be a laugh riot; it's just a question of modulation, of balancing the loud yuks and cruel jabs with some delicate feeling, mixing a real face in with the cartoons."
Manohla Dargis

"What causes laughter is the sudden transformation of a tense expectation into nothing."
Immanuel Kant

"Never make people laugh. If you would succeed in life, you must be solemn, solemn as an ass."
James Garfield

MUSIC

"Music alone can abolish differences of language or culture between two people and evokes something indestructible within them."
Irene Nemirovsky

"Ah, music. A magic beyond all we do here."
Albus Dumbledore, in *Harry Potter and the Sorcerer's Stone* by *J. K. Rowling*

"You are either born a nightingale or a crow."
Louis Kaufman

"I would rather write 10,000 notes than a single letter of the alphabet."
  Ludwig van Beethoven

"The music is not in the notes, but in the silence between."
  Wolfgang Amadeus Mozart

PHOTOGRAPHS AND PHOTOGRAPHY

"You don't make a photograph just with a camera. You bring to the act of photography all the pictures you have seen, the books you have read, the music you have heard, the people you have loved."
  Ansel Adams

"We think of photographs as the captured past. But some photographs are like DNA. In them you can read your whole future."
  Anne Michaels

"What the Photograph reproduces to infinity has occurred only once: the Photograph mechanically repeats what could never be repeated existentially."
  Roland Barthes

"In every old photograph lurks catastrophe."
  Roger Cohen

SPORTS

"Sports serve society by providing vivid examples of excellence."
  George F. Will

"The sports pages report men's triumphs and the front page seems always to be reporting their failures. I prefer to read about men's triumphs than their failures."
Earl Warren

"Champions keep playing until they get it right."
Billie Jean King

"It ain't about how hard you can hit. It's about how hard you can *get* hit, and keep moving forward."
Sylvester Stallone, in *Rocky Balboa*

"When you're riding, only the race in which you're riding is important."
Bill Shoemaker

"The only way to prove that you're a good sport is to lose."
Ernie Banks

"Something constructive comes from every defeat."
Tom Landry

"It ain't over 'til it's over."
Yogi Berra

TABLE TENNIS

"You have to play good to be lucky."
Atanda Musa

"Ping Pong is a lifestyle, a training in attention, a diversion, a mad passion and a way of not taking anything too seriously and taking some tiny things much too seriously. The only injuries I've had, playing it, are to pride, sang-froid and self-love."

Pico Iyer

"You can't lose if you keep the ball on the table."

Atanda Musa

TELEVISION

"TV and the movies have spoiled the most intimate moments of our lives. They have given us conventions which dominate our expectations in instants whose intensity would ordinarily make them spontaneous and unique. We have conventions of grief, which we learned from the Kennedys, and ordained gestures for victory by which we imitate the athletes we see on the tube, who in turn have learned the same things from other jocks they saw on TV."

Scott Turow

"I find television very educational. Every time someone turns on the set, I go into the other room and read a book."

Groucho Marx

"Television enables you to be entertained in your home by people you wouldn't have in your home."

David Frost

"Television has proved that people will look at anything rather than each other."

Ann Landers

"Television is called a medium because so little of it is rare or well done."

Fred Allen

TRANSLATION

"Translation is a kind of transubstantiation; one poem becomes another. You can choose your philosophy of translation just as you choose how to live: the free adaptation that sacrifices detail to meaning, the strict crib that sacrifices meaning to exactitude. The poet moves from life to language, the translator moves from language to life; both, like the immigrant, try to identify the invisible, what's between the lines, the mysterious implications."

Anne Michaels

"To translate is to decode: to transpose one mode of thinking, feeling, fearing, appraising, into the word patterns of another. No language can be separated from its psychological skin, or its sociological garments. Languages are acculturated verbalizations of experience and thought."

Leo Rosten

"Reading poetry in translation is like kissing a woman through a veil."

Chaim Nachman Bialik

WRITERS AND WRITING

"You learn to write by writing, not thinking about it. Don't wait for the Muse to tap you on the shoulder."

Frank Herbert

"Writing is never fun."

E. B. White

"The wastepaper basket is a writer's best friend."
Isaac Bashevis Singer

"Write without pay until somebody offers to pay you. If nobody offers within three years, sawing wood is what you were intended for."
Mark Twain

"No man but a blockhead ever wrote except for money."
Samuel Johnson

"If writing must be a precise form of communication, it should be treated like a precision instrument. It should be sharpened, and it should not be used carelessly."
Theodore M. Bernstein

"Nothing stinks like a pile of unpublished writing, which remark I guess shows I still don't have a pure motive (O it's-such-fun-I-just-can't-stop-who-cares-if-it's-published-or-read) about writing . . . I still want to see it finally ritualized in print."
Sylvia Plath

"I can shake off everything if I write; my sorrows disappear; my courage is reborn."
Anne Frank

"Writing fiction is like going out on an adventure. Writing non-fiction involves describing an adventure you've already had."
Etgar Keret

"I have finished my play, now all I have to do is write it down."
Alexandre Dumas

"The best way to become acquainted with a subject is to write a book about it."
   Benjamin Disraeli

"Words are acts. Through writing, one can change history."
   Mario Vargas Llosa

"Your last piece is never going to write your next one for you."
   John McPhee

"Writing a book—assuming you have a minimal level of intelligence—is just a matter of sitting down."
   Martin Garbus

"You are not what you write, but what you have read."
   Jorge Luis Borges

"When all is said and done, the writer may realize that he has wasted his youth and wrecked his health for nothing."
   T. S. Eliot

"The conscious mind is the editor, and the subconscious mind is the writer."
   Steve Martin

"People are interested only in themselves. If a story is not about the hearer, he will not listen. And here I make a rule—a great and lasting story is about everyone or it will not last. The strange and foreign is not interesting—only the deeply personal and familiar."
   John Steinbeck

"The easiest decision a reader can make is to stop reading. This means that every sentence has to count in grabbing the reader's attention, starting with the first."
   Bret Stephens

"You don't finish writing a book. You stop writing it."
   Benjamin Dreyer

"The hardest thing about writing is writing."
   Nora Ephron

Government, Politics, and Power

"Power is nothing unless you can turn it into influence."

Condoleezza Rice

"Mothers all want their sons to grow up to be president, but they don't want them to become politicians in the process."

John F. Kennedy

BUREAUCRACY

"Bureaucracies never do what is best when they can do what is safe."

Tom Coburn

"Bureaucracy defends the status quo long past the time when the quo has lost its status."

Lawrence J. Peter

"A memorandum is written not to inform the reader but to protect the writer."

Dean Acheson

"When enough bureaucratic prestige has been invested in a policy, it is easier to see it fail than to abandon it."

Henry A. Kissinger

DEMOCRACY

"Democracy is the worst form of government except for all those others that have been tried."

Winston Churchill

"Hain't we got all the fools in town on our side? And ain't that a big enough majority in any town?"

The King, in *The Adventures of Huckleberry Finn* by *Mark Twain*

"In all true democracies, elections legitimize the system not merely through the casting of votes, but through the process itself, the self-renewing exchange of hopes and promises, demands and compromises, that make up the flawed miracle of democracy."
Shashi Tharoor

"The vote is the most powerful nonviolent change agent you have in a democratic society. You must use it because it is not guaranteed."
John R. Lewis

"Elections are a door to democracy. They are not democracy."
Shimon Peres

"Beware the fury of an aroused democracy."
Dwight D. Eisenhower

"Democracy is only a theory that doesn't mean very much when people live in fear."
Rudy Giuliani

"Democracies tend to ignore, even deny, threats to their existence because they loathe doing what is necessary to counter them."
Jean-Francois Revel

"The most basic test of democracy is not what people do when they win; it is what people do when they lose. Citizens bring their deepest passions to a public debate—convictions they regard as morally self-evident. Democracy means the possibility of failure. Respecting the temporary outcome of a democratic process is the definition of political maturity."
Michael Gerson

"A dictator speaks only for himself, while 'the people' are transformed, through force and fear, into an abstraction, an instrument, a rhetorical trope. On the contrary, it is only in a democracy where the government can morally and lawfully be said to speak for the people, since it was morally and lawfully chosen by the people to speak for them."

Bret Stephens

"You measure a democracy by the freedom it gives its dissidents, not the freedom it gives its assimilated conformists."

Abbie Hoffman

"The success of democracy comes not from its leaders doing extraordinary things, but from its citizens doing ordinary things extraordinarily well."

John Gardner

"I don't care who does the electing as long as I do the nominating."

William Marcy "Boss" Tweed

"The best argument against democracy is a five-minute conversation with the average voter."

Winston Churchill

"Democracy is hearing a knock on your front door early in the morning and knowing that it's only the milkman."

Felipe Gonzalez

"This country, with its institutions, belongs to the people who inhabit it. Whenever they grow weary of the existing Government, they can exercise their constitutional right of amending it, or their revolutionary right to dismember or overthrow it."

Abraham Lincoln

GOVERNMENT

"The equal rights of man, and the happiness of every individual, are now acknowledged to be the only legitimate objects of government."

   Thomas Jefferson

"Nothing can destroy a government more quickly than its failure to observe its own laws, or worse, its disregard of the charter of its own existence."

   Tom Clark

"There are no necessary evils in government. Its evils exist only in its abuses. If it would confine itself to equal protection, and, as Heaven does its rains, shower its favors alike on the high and the low, the rich and the poor, it would be an unqualified blessing."

   Andrew Jackson

"If the Government becomes a lawbreaker, it breeds contempt for law; it invites every man to become a law unto himself; it invites anarchy."

   Louis D. Brandeis

"When there is a lack of honor in government, the morals of the whole people are poisoned."

   Herbert Hoover

"The challenge in Washington was not getting a job, but figuring out what to do with it."

   David Kessler

"You campaign in poetry. You govern in prose."
Mario Cuomo

NATIONALISM

"Without a country of your own, you have neither name, voice, nor rights nor admission as brothers into the fellowship of peoples. You are the bastards of humanity."
Giuseppe Mazzini

"We have created Italy. Now all we need to do is to create Italians."
Massimo Taparelli D'Azeglio

"The nation, like the individual, is the culmination of a long past of endeavors, sacrifice and devotion. A heroic past, great men, glory, this is the social capital upon which one bases a national idea. To have common glories in the past and to have a common will in the present; to have performed great deeds together, to wish to perform still more—these are the essential conditions for being a people. More valuable by far than common customs posts and frontiers conforming to strategic ideas is the fact of sharing, in the past, a glorious heritage and regrets, and of having, in the future, a program to put into effect, or the fact of having suffered, enjoyed and hoped together."
Ernest Renan

"National movements are often carried away by delirium. Their politics can become deeds of self-immolation."
Fouad Ajami

POLITICAL CAMPAIGNS

"Your opponent can't talk when he has your fist in his mouth."
Bill Clinton

"You don't win by just being against things. You only win by being for things and making your message perfectly clear."
Margaret Thatcher

"Sadly, if you have enough time and enough money, anyone's reputation can be destroyed."
Mark Kirk

"Today they blacken your character, tomorrow they blacken your boots."
Benjamin Disraeli

"The problem in politics is this: You don't get any credit for disaster averted. Going to the voters and saying, 'Boy, things really suck. But you know what? If it wasn't for me, they would suck worse.' That is not a platform on which anybody has ever gotten elected in the history of the world."
Barney Frank

"People who run for public office put themselves in a position in which everybody is inclined to believe the worst about them. The things that are ripe for ridicule become famous. The accomplishments fade from view. The cynics of the world, which includes almost everybody when it comes to politics, write you off as a sleazeball because it feels so good and superior to do so."
David Brooks

"The problem with political science is that it is not science. Each election is different."
   Jonathan S. Tobin

"Never murder a man who is committing suicide."
   Woodrow Wilson

POLITICAL PARTIES

"Ruling parties and presidencies are almost never felled by issues alone. Rather, it is the more general perception of creeping chaos—the sense that the leaders no longer have a firm grasp on events or the credibility to unite disparate constituencies that causes political powers to come undone."
   Matt Bai

"When a third party's demands become popular enough, they are appropriated by one or both of the major parties and the third party disappears. Third parties are like bees: Once they have stung, they die."
   Richard Hofstadter

"Our children are initiated into faction before they know their right hand from their left. They no sooner begin to speak but 'Whig' and 'Tory' are the first words that they learn. They are taught in their infancy to hate one half of the nation, and contract all the violence and passion of a party before they come to use their reason."
   Joseph Addison (1716)

POLITICIANS

"The political mind is the product of men in political life who have been twice spoiled. They have been spoiled with praise and they have been spoiled with abuse. With them, nothing is natural, everything is artificial."

Calvin Coolidge

"All political lives, unless they are cut off in midstream at a happy juncture, end in failure."

Enoch Powell

"It is in the nature of politics that all the elements that ultimately bring about the downfall are there from the outset, albeit in mild form. Time merely enlarges and strengthens them."

Tony Blair

"Our democracy, at least as it has evolved, takes individuals who are reasonable in private and it churns them through a public process that is almost tailor-made to undermine their virtues. The process of perpetually kissing up to the voters destroys the leadership qualities the voters are looking for in the first place: tranquility of spirit, independence of mind and a sensitivity to the contours and complexity of reality."

David Brooks

"Perfection in candidates is obtainable in the same place where imaginary friends reside. What we can hope to actually find in the real world, if we're fortunate, are individuals of proven skill and talent, who embody integrity, and whose agenda is anchored in and draws strength from American ideals."

Paul Singer

"A politician is like a spring flower: He blossoms, he blooms, and a time comes for him to fade."

Zulfikar Ali Bhutto

"Never complain and never explain."

Benjamin Disraeli

"If you want to get elected, learn to speak. If you want to stay elected, learn to listen."

Tom Daschle

"Once you catch Presidentitis, there's only one antidote: formaldehyde."

Congressman Morris K. Udall

"To be a successful Congressman, one must have the friendliness of a child, the enthusiasm of a teen-ager, the assurance of a college boy, the diplomacy of a wayward husband, the curiosity of a cat, and the good humor of an idiot."

Congressman Emanuel Celler

"The way to succeed in politics is by talking to the people and voting for the special interests."

Senator Joseph Montoya

"Politicians strive to get a reputation for being brave without being brave."

Holman W. Jenkins, Jr.

"Mothers all want their sons to grow up to be president, but they don't want them to become politicians in the process."

John F. Kennedy

"Be wary of the authorities! They do not befriend anyone unless it serves their own needs. They appear as a friend when it is to their advantage, but do not stand by a person in his hour of need."

Gamliel, in *Teachings of the Fathers*

POLITICIANS AND MEDIA

"The press is never on the side of the government. Whatever the government does, the press believes it can do it better."

Shimon Peres

"The fundamental rule is to shoehorn what you want to say into the answer no matter what the question is."

George Stephanopoulos

"If you don't say anything, they can't quote you."

Calvin Coolidge

POLITICS

"They are wrong who think that politics is like an ocean voyage or a military campaign, something to be done with some particular end in view, something which leaves off as soon as that end is reached. It is not a public chore, to be got over with. It is a way of life."

Plutarch

"In politics, the first thing is to continue to exist."

Ernest Hemingway

"Procedure, precedent and tradition exist for good reason; ignoring and undermining them blazes a path to political disorder."

John Podhoretz

"The central conservative truth is that it is culture, not politics, that determines the success of a society. The central liberal truth is that politics can change a culture and save it from itself."
Daniel Patrick Moynihan

"Controversy builds political stature."
Edmund Morris, in *The Rise of Theodore Roosevelt*

"It is the curse of politics that in certain cases monstrous acts of impurity may be the acts most moral given the paucity of alternatives. But it is always possible instead to preserve one's own purity and allow the world to fall into ruin."
Yoram Hazony

"It is in the nature of political life that 1) its most decisive moments always involve a choice of evils; 2) choosing the lesser evil still involves choosing an evil; and, 3) most important, one can never know with certainty that the choice made was, in fact, the lesser evil."
Bret Stephens

"The first thing you do is get loyal people. Competence is a bonus."
Lyn Nofziger

"Politics that is divorced from reality is not politics; it's self-indulgence, a charade. Those with a proper grasp of politics understand that life is complicated, that many of our problems are complex and daunting, and that dramatic change is rare and rarely easy. They know we live in a broken world where things often go wrong, expectations need to be tempered, our grasp of truth and knowledge is incomplete and perfection is always beyond our grasp."
Peter Wehner

"Politics is a contact sport. If you don't like it, keep your uniform off."
Bill Clinton

"Political life must be taken as you find it."
Benjamin Disraeli

POLITICS AND MONEY

"There are two things that are important in politics. The first is money and I can't remember what the second is."
Mark Hanna

"Both Republican and Democratic pols define capitalism as a system with economic activity sufficient to produce campaign contributions."
Daniel Henninger

"Money chases momentum."
Josh Kraushaar

POWER

"The only prize much cared for by the powerful is power. The prize of the general is not a bigger tent, but command."
Oliver Wendell Holmes, Jr.

"It is much safer to be feared than to be loved when one of the two must be lacking."
Niccolo Machiavelli

"Power concedes nothing without a demand."
Frederick Douglass

"At the banquet table of nature, there are no reserved seats. You get what you can take, and you keep what you can hold. If you can't take anything, you won't get anything, and if you can't hold anything, you won't keep anything. And you can't take anything without organization."
A. Philip Randolph

"Purity requires that man renounce power; but morality requires that man have power in order to pursue right."
Yoram Hazony

"You can have the best car in town, but it won't go anywhere if you don't put your foot on the pedal."
Mark Steyn

"Power is nothing unless you can turn it into influence."
Condoleezza Rice

"Power tends to corrupt and absolute power absolutely."
Lord Acton

"Power corrupts—that has been said and written so often that it has become a cliché. But what is never said, but is just as true, is that power *reveals*. When a man is climbing, trying to persuade others to give him power, he must conceal those traits that might make others reluctant to give it to him, that might even make them refuse to give it to him. Once the man has power, it is no longer necessary for him to hide those traits."
Robert Caro

"Proximity to the power deludes some into believing they wield it."

Beau Willimon

"If you think you're too small to have an impact, try going to bed with a mosquito in the room."

Dalai Lama

"A sinking world power is the heaviest lift imaginable. Ask Winston Churchill."

Daniel Henninger

"If we know anything, it is that weakness is provocative."

Donald Rumsfeld

"What do people with power want? More power."

Oracle, in *The Matrix Reloaded* by *Andy* and *Larry Wachowski*

REVOLUTION

"A revolution is not the same as inviting people to dinner or writing an essay or painting a picture or doing fancy needlework. It cannot be anything so refined, so calm and gentle, so mild, kind, courteous, restrained and magnanimous. A revolution is an uprising, an act of violence whereby one class overthrows another."

Mao Zedong

"Revolutions are not made. They come. A revolution is as natural as an oak. It comes out of the past. Its foundations are laid back in history."

Wendell Phillips

"So long as we read about revolutions in books, they all look very nice—like those landscapes which, as artistic engravings on white vellum, look so pure and friendly: dung heaps engraved on copper do not smell, and the eye can easily wade through an engraved morass."

Heinrich Heine

"One must open men's eyes, not tear them out."

Alexander Herzen, to Mikhail Bakunin

"The Revolution began in the minds of Americans long before any shots were fired or blood shed."

John Adams

"Revolutions by their nature attract the misfits and losers of life's lottery. The status quo, by contrast, wins the loyalty of the secure and well-favored, who often project a strength of character that masks their incapacity. Even the most incompetent—Marie Antoinette or Czar Nicholas II—end up looking nobler than their revolutionary tormentors."

Arthur Herman

"A nation-state wants concrete things such as demarcated borders, markets, access to natural resources, security, influence, and, of course, stability—all things that could be negotiated with other nation-states. A revolution, on the other hand, doesn't want anything in particular because it wants everything."

Amir Taheri

"In retrospect, all revolutions seem inevitable. Beforehand, all revolutions seem impossible."

Michael McFaul

"All successful revolutions are the kicking in of a rotten door."
John Kenneth Galbraith

SOCIALISM

"Instead of believing that happy, successful individuals make for a successful society, socialism insists that a perfectly functioning system will produce happy individuals. When the system comes first, the individual becomes an afterthought."
Garry Kasparov

"The inherent vice of capitalism is the unequal sharing of blessings; the inherent virtue of socialism is the equal sharing of miseries."
Winston Churchill

"The trouble with socialism is that eventually you run out of other people's money."
Margaret Thatcher

"Compassion is not weakness, and concern for the unfortunate is not socialism."
Hubert H. Humphrey

SOVEREIGNTY

"A state is not handed to a people on a silver platter."
Chaim Weizmann

"Sovereignty entails obligations. One is not to massacre your own people. Another is not to support terrorism in any way. If a government fails to meet these obligations, then it forfeits some of the normal advantages of sovereignty, including the right to be left alone inside your own territory."

Richard Haass

"Better to reign in hell than to serve in heaven."

John Milton, in *Paradise Lost*

SECTION 8

Money and Business

"Things of value come only after hard work."
Socrates

"Money itself isn't bad or good. Money itself doesn't have power or not have power. It is our interpretation of money, our interaction with it, where the real mischief is and where we find the real opportunity for self-discovery and personal transformation."
Lynne Twist

BUSINESS

"There is only one boss. The customer. And he can fire everybody in the company from the chairman on down simply by spending his money somewhere else."
Sam Walton

"If a man in one lifetime is responsible for creating one hundred real jobs, permanent jobs, then he's done more than most do-gooders have ever achieved."
Phil Gramm

"Business is the ultimate game, in which you keep score with money."
Nolan K. Bushnell, founder of Atari

"Take away all my steel mills. Take away all my money. Leave me my people, and in five years I will have everything back."
Andrew Carnegie

"Every time somebody buys your company, they want you to stay, you want to stay and then all of a sudden you don't. You want out and they want you out."
Michael Bloomberg

"We did not waste a moment drafting a partnership agreement. Important relationships in life require neither pen and ink nor red seal. Their terms are written in spirit."
Morris L. Ernst

"It is not true that high wages make for prosperity. Instead, prosperity makes high wages."
Albert Wiggin

"A man who knows he's making money for other people ought to get some of the profit he brings in. Don't make any difference if it's baseball or a bank or a vaudeville show. It's a business, I tell you. There ain't no sentiment to it. Forget that stuff."
Babe Ruth

"You can't do a good deal with a bad person."
Warren Buffett

CAPITALISM

"Capitalism is the extraordinary belief that the nastiest of men for the nastiest of motives will somehow work for the benefit of us all."
John Maynard Keynes

"Companies come and go. It's part of the genius of capitalism."
Paul O'Neill

"Nobody spends somebody else's money as carefully as he spends his own. Nobody uses somebody else's resources as carefully as he uses his own. So, if you want efficiency and effectiveness, if you want knowledge to be properly utilized, you have to do it through the means of private property."
Milton Friedman

"Only capitalists can destroy capitalism."
Felix G. Rohatyn

"Some see private enterprise as a predatory target to be shot, others as a cow to be milked, but few are those who see it as a sturdy horse pulling the wagon."
Winston Churchill

"The most important single central fact about a free market is that no exchange takes place unless both parties benefit."
Milton Friedman

"Capitalism takes more people out of poverty than aid."
Bono

EXPERTS

"All the experts are experts on what was. There are no experts on what will be."
David Ben-Gurion

"There are no experts, only personal opinions."
Jason Greenblatt

"Nobody knows anything."
William Goldman

INVESTING AND INVESTMENTS

"Be fearful when others are greedy, and be greedy when others are fearful."
Warren Buffett

"October. This is one of the peculiarly dangerous months to speculate in stocks in. The others are July, January, September,

April, November, May, March, June, December, August and February."

Mark Twain

"Investing should be more like watching paint dry or watching grass grow. If you want excitement, take $800 and go to Las Vegas."

Paul Samuelson

"The dumbest reason in the world to buy a stock is because it's going up."

Warren Buffett

"Bubbles always end, and almost always end badly. There is always some supposed reason that 'this time is different,' but it never is."

Ben Stein

"I made my money by selling too soon."

Bernard M. Baruch

JOURNALISM

"With a circulation of a few hundred, you could change the world."

Irving Kristol

"The only time a reporter is ever, ever properly the adversary of his news source is when the news source refuses to cooperate in the transmission of information that belongs in the public domain."

Roy Fisher

"I don't care if my reporters seek the late night companionship of elephants as long as they don't cover the circus."
A. M. Rosenthal

"Journalists cannot serve two masters. To the extent that they take on the task of suppressing information or biting their tongue for the sake of some political agenda, they are betraying the trust of the public and corrupting their own profession."
Thomas Sowell

"If it's big, hit it."
Bill Mauldin

"If you don't read the newspaper, you are uninformed. If you do read the newspaper, you are misinformed."
Mark Twain

LAWYERS

"To whom, if not the lawyer, may we look for guidance in solving the problems of a sorely stricken society?"
Harlan F. Stone

"If he would be a great lawyer, he must first consent to be a great drudge."
Daniel Webster

"A lawyer's chief business is to keep his clients out of litigation."
Elihu Root

"Law school is simply a thing to be endured, tolerated, lived through, bitched about, and quickly forgotten. This three-year sojourn among the big brown books is a severe rite of passage and an exorbitantly expensive investment. It is no longer a wonder to me that men and women march out of these places hoping to milk corporations or do unmentionable things to the poor."

Pat Conroy

"God works wonders now and then; behold, a lawyer, an honest man."

Benjamin Franklin

MONEY

"Money itself isn't bad or good. Money itself doesn't have power or not have power. It is our interpretation of money, our interaction with it, where the real mischief is and where we find the real opportunity for self-discovery and personal transformation."

Lynne Twist

"To turn $100 into $110 is work. To turn $100 million into $110 million is inevitable."

Edgar Bronfman

"I don't want to be a millionaire. I just want to live like one."

Toots Shor

"Rich or poor, it's good to have money."

Benjamin Siegel

"Beyond an amount necessary to live in modest comfort, money is not that important, and often more of a burden than a pleasure."

Ben Stein

"Focusing your life solely on making a buck shows a certain poverty of ambition."
Barack Obama

"The older you get, the less time you want to spend doing stuff for money."
Richard Price

"Everyone is cheap about something."
Rachel Ringler

"For money, you can have everything it is said. No, that is not true. You can buy food, but not appetite; medicine, but not health; soft beds, but not sleep; knowledge but not wisdom; glitter, but not beauty; fun, but not joy; acquaintances, but not friends; servants, but not faithfulness; gray hair, but not honor; leisure, but not peace. For money, you can have the husk of all things. But not the kernel. That cannot be had for money."
Arne Garborg

"There is no dignity quite so impressive and no independence quite so important as living within your means."
Calvin Coolidge

"When somebody says it's not about the money, it's about the money."
H. L. Mencken

POSSESSIONS

"Life is not a having and a getting, but a being and a becoming."
Matthew Arnold

"More possessions, more worries."
Hillel, in *Teachings of the Fathers*

"Material things are so vulnerable to the humiliations of decay."
Marilynne Robinson

"It's no accident that most ads are pitched to people in their 20s and 30s. Not only are they so much cuter than their elders, but they are less likely to have gone through the transformative process of cleaning out their deceased parents' stuff. Once you go through that, you can never look at *your* stuff in the same way. You start to look at your stuff a little postmortemistically."
Roz Chast

"You only truly possess that which you cannot lose in a shipwreck."
Abu Hamid al-Ghazali

PROPERTY

"The property of others should be as precious to you as your own."
Yossi, in *Teachings of the Fathers*

"In the history of the world, no one has ever washed a rented car."
Lawrence Summers

PUBLICITY

"Noise is everything! A sustained noise in itself is a remarkable fact. All of world history is nothing but clamor: clamor of arms, clamor of ideas on the march. One must make use of the noise and yet despise it."

Theodor Herzl

"Since we cannot change reality, let us change the eyes which see reality."

Nikos Kazantzakis

"Men are rewarded or punished not for what they do, but rather how their acts are defined. This is why men are more interested in better justifying themselves than in better behaving themselves."

Thomas Szasz

"Publicity is like eating peanuts. Once you start, you can't stop."

Andy Warhol

TAXES

"Anyone may so arrange his affairs so that his taxes shall be as low as possible; he is not bound to choose that pattern which will best pay the Treasury; there is not even a patriotic duty to increase one's taxes."

Learned Hand

"The art of taxation consists in so plucking the goose as to get the most feathers with the least hissing."

Jean-Baptiste Colbert

"The estate tax is a very legitimate claim of society on an accumulation of wealth which would not have occurred without an orderly market, free education and incredible dollars spent on research."

William H. Gates, Sr.

"I like to pay taxes. With them I buy civilization."
    Oliver Wendell Holmes, Jr.

TRADE

"Every man lives by exchanging."
    Adam Smith

"Trade cannot exist without trust, and it is very difficult to trust strangers."
    Yuval Noah Harari

"Open economies and free trade are negatively correlated with genocide and war."
    Steven Pinker

"It is the maxim of every prudent master of a family, never to attempt to make at home what it will cost him more to make than to buy. . . . If a foreign country can supply us with a commodity cheaper than we ourselves can make it, better buy it of them."
    Adam Smith

"When trade stops, war comes."
    Jack Ma

UNIONS

"The capitalists cannot exterminate a real labor organization by fighting it. They are only dangerous when they fraternize with it."
    Vincent St. John

"When the unions are fully satisfied with a state or society, this is a sure sign that the unions are worthless."
 Helmut Schmidt

"Public-sector collective bargaining is an inherently corrupt process. Unions spend their members' dues to help elect the politicians who sit on the other side of the bargaining table. Thus, the very officeholders who are supposed to be representing the interests of the taxpayer are often beholden to their putative adversaries, whom they assist in looting the public treasury."
 James Taranto

WEALTH

"The way to wealth, if you desire it, is as plain as the way to market. It depends chiefly on two words, industry and frugality. That is, waste neither time nor money, but make the best use of both."
 Benjamin Franklin

"Sound investing can make you very wealthy if you're not in too big of a hurry. And it never makes you poor, which is better."
 Warren Buffett

"Who is the wealthy one? The person satisfied with his lot in life."
 Ben Zoma, in *Teachings of the Fathers*

"Be thankful for what you have; you'll end up having more. If you concentrate on what you don't have, you will never, ever have enough."
 Oprah Winfrey

"Even Rothschild, with all his money, can't arrange to have a view of the sea from a window in Jerusalem."
   Meir Shalev

WORK

"I'm a great believer in jobs for teens. They teach important life lessons, build character, and inflict just the right amount of humiliation necessary for future success in the working world."
   Gillian Flynn

"Things of value come only after hard work."
   Socrates

"I never heard of 9 to 5. Anyone who works those hours and expects to succeed is a dumbbell."
   Lawrence Valenstein

"The less you do, the less you are able to do."
   Rachel Ringler

SECTION 9

The Dark Side

"The real hell of life is that everyone has his reasons."
   Jean Renoir

"Keep a light, hopeful heart. But expect the worst."
   Joyce Carol Oates

ANGER

"Anyone can become angry, that is easy; but to be angry with the right person, to the right degree, at the right time, for the right purpose and in the right way, that is not easy."

Aristotle

"Rage destroys our moral compass—and allows us to be manipulated by those who want us to lose our way."

Arnold E. Resnicoff

"Beyond anger lies despair, the emotion which accompanies the belief in the hopelessness of one's cause, and the powerlessness of one's self."

Yoram Hazony

"Any person capable of angering you becomes your master."

Epictetus

"Don't get mad, get even."

Robert F. Kennedy

ANTI-SEMITISM

"Judaeophobia is an unfailing prognosis of barbarism and collapse, and the states and movements that promulgate it are doomed to suicide as well as homicide."

Christopher Hitchens

"The hate that begins with Jews never ends with Jews."
Jonathan Sacks

"Anti-Semitism never sees itself as a hatred; it views itself as a revelation. An attack on the Jew is never offensive; it is always defensive."
Edward Rothstein

"Zionism is part of the Jewish religion. It is the expression of nationalism of the Jewish people. To reject Zionism is to deny Jews the right to nationhood and the right to peoplehood."
I. L. Kenen

"When people criticize Zionism, they mean Jews—make no mistake about it."
Martin Luther King, Jr.

APPEASEMENT

"Appeasement is a vote to live in the present tense, to hold the comforts of the moment. To fight for King and country is to fight for the future."
Mark Steyn

"No people in history have ever survived who thought they could protect their freedom by making themselves inoffensive to their enemies."
Dean Acheson

"Appeasement in the name of *realpolitik* only encourages would-be dictators. And such moral weakness inevitably leads to very real costs in human life."
Garry Kasparov

"The key lesson of the 1930s is that appeasement leads directly to war."
Mark Kirk

"An appeaser is one who feeds a crocodile—hoping it will eat him last."
Winston Churchill

CORRUPTION

"Anyone in a position of power is either corrupt or assumed to be corrupt, and the assumption of corruption is as bad as the reality of it."
Stanley A. McChrystal

"Corruption is the result of a decadent political regime. It is the main cause of social and economic inequality."
Andrés Manuel López Obrador

"Themes of crime and political corruption are always relevant."
Martin Scorsese

"Fighting corruption is not a one-night affair."
Olusegun Obasanjo

COWARDICE

"A civilization is not destroyed by wicked people; it is not necessary that people be wicked but only that they be spineless."
James Baldwin

"To know what is right and not to do it is the worst cowardice."
Confucius

"Being afraid you'll look like a coward is the worst reason for doing anything."

John Irving

"Courage is often lack of insight, whereas cowardice in many cases is based on good information."

Peter Ustinov

DICTATORS

"There is a fundamental difference between democratic leaders and dictators. Because democratic leaders are dependent on the will of the people, they strive to promote peace and prosperity, opting for war only as a last resort. By contrast, in dictatorships, external enemies become the dictator's life blood, enabling him to divert discontent with his own repressive rule."

Natan Sharansky

"Dictators consistently underestimate the strength of democracies, and democracies provoke war through their love of peace, which the dictators mistake for weakness."

Joshua Muravchik

"It is enough that the people know there was an election. The people who cast the votes decide nothing. The people who count the votes decide everything."

Joseph Stalin

"A state that denies its citizens their basic rights becomes a danger to its neighbors as well: internal arbitrary rule will be reflected in arbitrary external relations. The suppression of public opinion, the abolition of public competition for power and its public exercise opens the way for the state power to arm itself in any way it sees fit. A state that does not hesitate to lie to its own people will not hesitate to lie to other states."

Václav Havel

"Don't say yes until I'm finished talking."

Darryl F. Zanuck

EVIL

"It's not in our hands to defeat evil. It's in our hands to limit it."

Joschka Fischer

"The line separating good and evil passes not through states, nor between classes, nor between political parties either, but right through every human heart, and through all human hearts. This line shifts. Inside us, it oscillates with the years. Even within hearts overwhelmed by evil, one small bridgehead of good is retained; and even in the best of all hearts, there remains a small corner of evil."

Alexander Solzhenitsyn

"In dictatorships, you need courage to fight evil; in the free world, you need courage to see evil."

Natan Sharansky

"Indifference to evil is more insidious than evil itself; it is more universal, more contagious, more dangerous."

Abraham Joshua Heschel

HATE

"Others may hate you, but those who hate you don't win unless you hate them, and then you destroy yourself."

Richard Nixon

"Hate harms the hated, but it destroys the hater."

Jonathan Sacks

"I imagine one of the reasons people cling to their hates so stubbornly is because they sense, once hate is gone, they will be forced to deal with pain."

James Baldwin

"You can't hate the roots of a tree and not hate the tree."

Malcolm X

THE HOLOCAUST

"If others were struck by Nazi barbarism, the Jews nevertheless seem different—and not merely in their own eyes—because of all, they all were singled out for extermination as a people. They were singled out, not because of what they did, or refrained from doing, and not because of faith or politics, but simply because they were there, they existed."

Amos Elon

"The Nazi destruction process did not come out of a void; it was the culmination of a cyclical trend. The missionaries of Christianity had said in effect: You have no right to live among us as Jews. The secular rulers who followed had proclaimed: You have no right to live among us. The German Nazis at last decreed: You have no right to live. The German Nazis, then, did not discard the past; they built upon it. They did not begin a development; they completed it."

Raul Hilberg

"Eichmann and his cohorts did not randomly go from being ordinary men to being murderers. They traversed a path paved by

centuries of pervasive anti-Semitism. They 'knew' this road and, given the society in which they lived, it seemed true and natural."
Deborah E. Lipstadt

"The Holocaust is so big, the scale of it is so gigantic, so enormous, that it becomes easy to think of it as something mechanical. Anonymous. But everything that happened, happened because someone made a decision. To pull a trigger, to flip a switch, to close a cattle car door, to hide, to betray."
Daniel Mendelsohn

"I'd like to call you all by name, but the list has been removed and there is nowhere else to look."
Anna Akhmatova

IMPRISONMENT

"When the prison gates slam behind an inmate, he does not lose his human quality; his mind does not become closed to ideas; his intellect does not cease to feed on a free and open interchange of opinions; his yearning for self-respect does not end; nor is his quest for self-realization concluded."
Thurgood Marshall

"A great poet might possibly be able to express the numbing evenness, the emptiness and helplessness, in short the intangible horror of imprisonment."
Albert Speer

"As I walked out the door toward the gate that would lead to my freedom, I knew if I didn't leave my bitterness and hatred behind, I'd still be in prison."
Nelson Mandela

INGRATITUDE

"Not to return one good office for another is inhuman; but to return evil for good is diabolical."
Seneca

"And there arose a new king over Egypt who knew not Joseph."
Exodus 1:8

"How could you blame the wind for carrying your kite?"
Cody Vichinsky

"If you pick up a starving dog and make him prosperous, he will not bite you. This is the principal difference between a dog and a man."
Mark Twain

NEUTRALITY

"The hottest fires of hell are reserved for those who in times of moral crisis are neutral."
Dante

"'Evenhandedness' is one of those unassailable words that pre-supposes that both sides are half-right and the way of wisdom is to split the difference. Occasionally, that is right; more often, justice lies closer to one side or the other."
William Safire

"We must always take sides. Neutrality helps the oppressor, never the victim."
Elie Wiesel

PESSIMISM AND PESSIMISTS

"Keep a light, hopeful heart. But expect the worst."
  Joyce Carol Oates

"I have observed that not the man who hopes when others despair, but the man who despairs when others hope, is admired by a large class of persons as a sage."
  John Stuart Mill

"The pessimism of the creative person is not decadence but a mighty passion for redemption of man."
  Isaac Bashevis Singer, in his Nobel Prize lecture

"Obstacles are what you see when you take your eyes off of the goal."
  Vince Lombardi

"A pessimist is an optimist with experience."
  Amos Yadlin

"There is hope—only not for us."
  Franz Kafka

PREJUDICE

"Prejudice, not being founded on reason, cannot be removed by argument."
  Samuel Johnson

"People are more susceptible to prejudice than to reason."
  Roger Ebert

"In the field of sports you are more or less accepted for what you do rather than what you are."
Althea Gibson

"There is no prejudice so strong as that which arises from a fancied exemption from all prejudice."
William Hazlitt

"If you are the pure, someone else needs to be impure."
Stacy Schiff

"It is very easy to hate. It is very difficult to justify hate."
Jonathan Sacks

RACISM

"At the heart of racism is the religious assertion that God made a creative mistake when He brought some people into being."
Friedrich Otto Hertz

"Accomplishments have no color."
Leontyne Price

"One day our descendants will think it incredible that we paid so much attention to things like the amount of melanin in our skin or the shape of our eyes or our gender instead of the unique identities of each of us as complex human beings."
Franklin Thomas

"There is no such thing as race. None. There is just a human race—scientifically, anthropologically."
Toni Morrison

"None of us is responsible for the complexion of his skin. This fact of nature offers no clue to the character or quality of the person underneath."
Marian Anderson

"No one is born hating another person because of the color of his skin, or his background, or his religion. People must learn to hate, and if they can learn to hate, they can be taught to love, for love comes more naturally to the human heart than its opposite."
Nelson Mandela

"Racism separates, but it never liberates. Hatred generates fear, and fear once given a foothold, binds, consumes and imprisons. Nothing is gained from prejudice. No one benefits from racism."
Thurgood Marshall

"I have a dream that my four little children will one day live in a nation where they will not be judged by the color of their skin but by the content of their character."
Martin Luther King, Jr.

RATIONALIZATION

"Transforming self-contempt into contempt for those you have failed is an old trick for soothing a bad conscience."
Russell Baker

"The real hell of life is that everyone has his reasons."
Jean Renoir

"It is easy to find a logical and virtuous reason for not doing what you don't want to do."
  John Steinbeck

"You gotta do what you gotta do."
  Bill Clinton

"Those who lack the courage will always find a philosophy to justify it."
  Albert Camus

SLAVERY

"Slaves are generally expected to sing as well as to work."
  Frederick Douglass

"The masters could not bring water to boil, harness to horse or strap their own drawers without us. We were better than them. We had to be. Sloth was literal death for us, while for them it was the whole ambition of their lives."
  Ta-Nehisi Coates

"Slavery is equally destructive to the master and the slave. For, whilst it stupefies the latter with fear, and reduces him below the condition of man, it brutalizes the former, by the practice of continual tyranny; and makes him the prey of all of the vices which render human nature loathsome."
  Charles Ball

"Slavery is the next thing to hell. If a person would send another into bondage, he would . . . be bad enough to send him into hell if he could."
  Harriet Tubman

"You can't hold a man down without staying down with him."
  Booker T. Washington

STUPIDITY

"Sometimes stupidity needs no other explanation."
  Eran Lerman

"The difference between genius and stupidity is that genius has its limits."
  Albert Einstein

"Who's the more foolish: The fool, or the fool who follows him?"
  George Lucas, in *Star Wars: The New Hope*

TERRORISM

"Any war is cruel and a curse, and sometimes civilians get hurt. But the difference between a soldier and a terrorist is that the former will do whatever is humanly possible to avoid civilian casualties, and the latter will plan it in advance."
  Menachem Begin

"The problem with threats like nuclear terror is that they are not solved but managed, not eliminated but faced, cut down to size and endured. . . . There is no single leap of technology, no grand strategic gambit or fortification that can render us completely secure against a determined terrorist. That is not an argument for doing nothing, but for doing many things at the same time, with the right degree of urgency and steadiness of purpose."
  Bill Keller

"Deterrence—the promise of massive retaliation against nations—means nothing against shadowy terrorist networks with no nation or citizens to defend."

George W. Bush

"The threat of global terrorism bent on mass slaughter means traditional civil liberty arguments are not so much wrong, as just made for another age."

Tony Blair

"International terrorism will take the place of human rights in our concern because it is the ultimate abuse of human rights."

Alexander Haig (1982)

TOTALITARIANISM

"The totalitarian phenomenon is not to be understood without making allowance for the thesis that some important part of every society consists of people who actively want tyranny: either to exercise it themselves or—much more mysteriously—to submit to it. Democracy will therefore always remain at risk."

Jean-François Revel

"The cardinal tenet of totalitarianism is that the masses must not be allowed to mass. Totalitarianism is a mortar and a pestle, grinding society to dust, atomizing individuals and assembling them only into compounds controlled by the state."

George F. Will

"While tyranny may ripen in certain political climates, it springs from sources deep within ourselves: the yearning for a politics without contradictions."

Bret Stephens

"Totalitarianism politicizes everything, so that neutrality is betrayal."
James Taranto

"For somehow this is tyranny's disease, to trust no friends."
Aeschylus

TRAGEDY

"When tragedies strike, we try to find someone to blame. And in the absence of a suitable candidate, we usually blame ourselves."
Julian Fellowes

"The tragedy of life is what dies inside a man while he lives."
Albert Schweitzer

"There is a difference between tragedy and atrocity. In tragedy what we learn compensates for the price of such knowledge. Atrocity offers no such balance or compensation, and thus no inner space in which to bury the event. At most, it leaves those of us left behind searching amidst the ashes to find meaning in an event of such magnitude that it defies our very sense of meaning."
Michael Berenbaum

WAR

"Never, never, never believe any war will be smooth and easy, or that anyone who embarks on the strange voyage can measure the tides and hurricanes he will encounter. The statesman who yields to war fever must realize that once the signal is given, he

is no longer the master of policy but the slave of unforeseeable and uncontrollable events."
   Winston Churchill

"Wars are easier to talk about than they are to fight."
   John F. Kennedy

"After every war
someone has to clean up.
Things won't
straighten themselves up, after all.

Someone has to push the rubble
to the side of the road,
so the corpse-filled wagons
can pass."
   Wisława Szymborska, from "The End and the Beginning"

"Great is the guilt of an unnecessary war."
   John Adams

"War's very objective is victory–not prolonged indecision. In war, indeed, there can be no substitute for victory."
   Douglas MacArthur

"There is a great inertia about all military operations of any size. But once this inertia has been overcome and movement is underway, they are almost as hard to arrest as to initiate."
   Ernest Hemingway

"War is nothing more than the continuation of politics by other means."
   Karl von Clausewitz

"In time of war, the laws fall silent."
Cicero

"Man has never developed a weapon he didn't eventually use."
Ronald Reagan

"In war, the latest refinements of science are linked with the cruelties of the Stone Age."
Winston Churchill

"War is the locomotive of history."
Karl Marx

"All warfare is based on deception. When able to attack, we must seem unable; when using our forces, we must seem inactive; when we are near, we must make the enemy believe we are far away."
Sun Tzu

"Hardships are part of war, and war is an aggregation of hardships. All citizens alike, both in and out of uniform, feel the impact of war in greater or lesser measure. Citizenship has its responsibilities as well as its privileges, and in time of war the burden is always heavier."
Hugo Black

"No bastard ever won a war by dying for his country. He won it by making the other poor dumb bastard die for his country."
George S. Patton

"The quickest way to end a war is to lose it."
George Orwell

"It is impossible to know war if you do not stand with the mass of the powerless caught in its maw. All narratives of war told through the lens of the combatants carry with them the seduction of violence. But once you cross to the other side, to stand in fear with the helpless and the weak, you confront the moral depravity of industrial slaughter and the scourge that is war itself."

Chris Hedges

"Only a fool or a fraud sentimentalizes war."

John McCain

SECTION 10

Our Fragile World

"Nature takes just as much cognizance of the deadly snake as of the greatest statesman."
Luther Burbank

"We do not inherit the earth from our ancestors. We borrow it from our children."
Chief Seattle

CIVILIZATION

"Civilization begins with order, grows with liberty, and dies with chaos."
Will Durant

"The history of our civilization, the great advances that made it possible, is not a story of cynics or doom criers. It is a gallant chronicle of the optimists, the determined people, men and women, who dreamed great dreams and dared to try whatever it took to make them come true."
Ronald Reagan

"The first human who hurled an insult instead of a stone was the founder of civilization."
Sigmund Freud

"Civilizations die from suicide, not murder."
Arnold J. Toynbee

ENDANGERED SPECIES

"Our prime purpose in this life is to help others. And if you can't help them, at least don't hurt them."
Dalai Lama

"Each and every animal on earth has as much right to be here as you and me."
Anthony Douglas Williams

"Animals are, like us, endangered species on an endangered planet, and we are the ones who are endangering them, it, and ourselves. They are innocent sufferers in a hell of our making."
    Jeffrey Moussaieff Masson

ENVIRONMENT

"We should not be over pleased with our victories over nature, since nature avenges itself for our victories."
    Friedrich Engels

"The nation behaves well if it treats the natural resources as assets which it must turn over to the next generation increased and not impaired in value."
    Theodore Roosevelt

"You can always measure the costs of environmental policy, but the benefits are harder to quantify. And of course, industry will always overstate the cost."
    Henry Waxman

"Whether we and our politicians know it or not, Nature is party to all our deals and decisions, and she has more votes, a longer memory, and a sterner sense of justice than we do."
    Wendell Berry

"Man is a part of nature, and his war against nature is inevitably a war against himself."
    Rachel Carson

"To Nature, the flea, the cockroach, the hyena, the buzzard, the cobra are as important as the dog who loves and guards you, the horse who understands and works for you, the young

girl in her lover's embrace, the child at its mother's knee in prayer, or the mature man on whom depend the happiness and well-being of a gracious wife and a family of lovely children."
  Luther Burbank

"We cannot say we love the land and then take steps to destroy it for use by future generations."
  John Paul II

"Rivers don't do anything; things are done to rivers."
  David Pargament

"We are such spendthrifts with our lives. The trick of living is to slip on and off the planet with the least fuss you can muster. We need to be like the farmer, who puts back into the soil what he takes out."
  Paul Newman

"Pollution should never be the price of prosperity."
  Al Gore

"We do not inherit the earth from our ancestors. We borrow it from our children."
  Chief Seattle

"We are living on this planet as if we had another one to go to."
  Terri Swearingen

FOOD

"The production of food, and not money, buys the division of labor that makes possible advance in civilization. It was not until the tillers of the soil produced more food than they themselves had need of that their fellow villagers were released for other tasks. Until food is available, the miner does not dig into the bowels of the earth for minerals and ore, and mechanics do not process ores and make the intricate machines of modern technology. There is no substitute for food in the complex division of labor in modern civilization."

Walter Clay Lowdermilk

"We can make a commitment to promote vegetables and fruits and whole grains on every part of every menu. We can make portion sizes smaller and emphasize quality over quantity. And we can help create a culture—imagine this—where our kids ask for healthy options instead of resisting them."

Michelle Obama

"Cheap industrial food is cheap only because the real costs of producing it are not reflected in the price at the checkout. Rather, those costs are charged to the environment, in the form of soil depletion and pollution; to the public purse, in the form of subsidies to conventional commodities farmers; to the public health, in the form of an epidemic of diabetes and obesity; and to the welfare of the farm-and food-factory workers, not to mention the well-being of the animals we eat."

Michael Pollan

HUNGER

"The day that hunger is eradicated from the earth, there will be the greatest spiritual explosion the world has ever known. Humanity cannot imagine the joy that will burst into the world on the day of that great revolution."

Federico García Lorca

"Men will sell all—their liberty and more—for food, if driven to this tragic choice."
Walter Clay Lowdermilk

"In the end they will lay their freedom at our feet and say to us, 'Make us your slaves, but feed us.'"
Fyodor Dostoyevsky

NATURE

"It is difficult to believe in the dreadful but quiet war of organic beings going on in the peaceful woods and smiling fields."
Charles Darwin

"In nature, nothing exists alone."
Rachel Carson

"Nature takes just as much cognizance of the deadly snake as of the greatest statesman."
Luther Burbank

"Nature has made up her mind that what cannot defend itself shall not be defended."
Ralph Waldo Emerson

"There is no such thing as bad weather, just bad clothing."
Swedish saying

"Landscapes of great wonder and beauty lie under our feet and all around us. . . . Life in these hidden worlds is more startling in reality than anything we can imagine. How could this earth

of ours, which is only a speck in the heavens, have so much variety of life, so many curious and exciting creatures?"
   Walt Disney

"Those who contemplate the beauty of the earth find reserves of strength that will endure as long as life lasts. There is something infinitely healing in the repeated refrains of nature—the assurance that dawn comes after night, and spring after winter."
   Rachel Carson

"Nature provides a free lunch, but only if we control our appetites."
   William Ruckelshaus

"Civilization can take us so far away from our true natures that we never know who we really are."
   Lawrence Wright

"Like music and art, love of nature is a common language that can transcend political or social boundaries."
   Jimmy Carter

"If we save our wild places, we will ultimately save ourselves."
   Steve Irwin

POVERTY

"Poverty is the worst form of violence."
   Mohandas Gandhi

"Poverty is not being able to protect your family. Poverty is not being able to save your children when mothers with more money could. And because the strongest instinct of a mother

is to protect her children, poverty is the most disempowering force on earth."
Melinda Gates

"Throughout history, poverty is the normal condition of man. Advances which permit this norm to be exceeded—here and there, now and then—are the work of an extremely small minority, frequently despised, often condemned, and almost always opposed by all right-thinking people. Whenever this tiny minority is kept from creating, or (as sometimes happens) is driven out of a society, the people then slip back into abject poverty."
Robert Heinlein

"Don't expect to build up the weak by pulling down the strong."
Calvin Coolidge

"Poverty is not an accident. Like slavery and apartheid, it is man-made and can be removed by the action of human beings."
Nelson Mandela

"Poverty entails fear and stress and sometimes depression. It means a thousand petty humiliations and hardships."
J. K. Rowling

SCIENCE

"Science knows no country, because knowledge belongs to humanity. It is the torch which illuminates the world."
Louis Pasteur

"Science is built of facts the way a house is built of bricks, but an accumulation of facts is no more science than a pile of bricks is a house."
Henri Poincaré

"A new [scientific] truth does not triumph by convincing its opponents, but because its opponents die, and a new generation grows up that is familiar with it."

Max Planck

"The good thing about science is that it's true whether or not you believe in it."

Neil deGrasse Tyson

"Men love to wonder, and that is the seed of science."

Ralph Waldo Emerson

TECHNOLOGY

"Truth is transient and there's no place where that truth is more transient than in technology. What was true about technology when you were a kid probably isn't true anymore."

Dean Kamen

"Before you become too entranced with gorgeous gadgets and mesmerizing video displays, let me remind you that information is not knowledge, knowledge is not wisdom, and wisdom is not foresight. Each grows out of the other, and we need them all."

Arthur C. Clarke

"We must work passionately and indefatigably to bridge the gulf between our scientific progress and our moral progress. One of the great problems of mankind is that we suffer from a poverty of the spirit which stands in glaring contrast to our scientific and technological abundance."

Martin Luther King, Jr.

"The human spirit must prevail over technology."
Albert Einstein

"We now expect more from technology and less from each other."
Sherry Turkle

"The Internet is like alcohol in some sense. It accentuates what you would do anyway. If you want to be a loner, you can be more alone. If you want to connect, it makes it easier to connect."
Esther Dyson

WATER

"You ain't gonna miss your water until your well runs dry."
Bob Marley

"When we think of water, we think of it as the air, infinite and inexhaustible."
Robert Glennon

"There isn't a scarcity of water. There is a scarcity of innovation."
Amir Peleg

"You don't have to be a scientist to understand that if you take more water out of the bathtub than you put into the bathtub, the bathtub will eventually go empty."
Tim Barnett

"Between earth and earth's atmosphere, the amount of water remains constant; there is never a drop more, never a drop less. This is a story of circular infinity, of a planet birthing itself."

Linda Hogan

"All the water that ever was, still is. We're drinking the same water as the dinosaurs drank."

Robert Glennon

"We have the ability to provide clean water for every man, woman and child on the earth. What has been lacking is the collective will to accomplish this."

Jean-Michel Cousteau

"Aquifers don't know about borders or politics or religion."

Humberto Yaakov

"When the well is dry, we learn the worth of water."

Benjamin Franklin

"As long as there is five percent more water than you need, no one notices it."

Stewart Resnick

"It never failed that during the dry years the people forgot the rich years, and during the wet years they lost all memory of the dry years. It was always that way."

John Steinbeck

"Nothing is more useful than water: but it will purchase scarcely anything; scarcely anything can be had in exchange for it."

Adam Smith

"Water is the main agricultural input. If it weren't, the Sahara would be green."

Antonio Nobre

"A civilization of faucet-turners can regard water supply indifferently. The generations of bucket-carriers and cloud watchers cannot."

Lyndon B. Johnson

"A person's ZIP Code should not determine the quality of the water they drink or the services they receive. People deserve to have clean water and clean waterways, no matter where they live."

George Hawkins

"The only alternative to water is water."

Danilo Turk

SECTION 11

Doing Good

"Nobody need wait a single moment before starting to improve the world."
Anne Frank

"Be ashamed to die until you have won some victory for humanity."
Horace Mann

CHARITY

"Charity that is a trifle to us can be precious to others."
Homer, in *The Odyssey*

"A good deed that comes easy to you is like a donation which does not cost you anything."
Abraham Cahan

"Those people favoring perpetual foundations argue that in the future there will most certainly be large and important societal problems that philanthropy will need to address. I agree. But there will then also be many super-rich individuals and families whose wealth will exceed that of today's Americans and to whom philanthropic organizations can make their case for funding. They should be able to allocate funds more rationally than a decedent six feet under will have ordained decades earlier."
Warren Buffett

"It's easy to offer someone something when you know he won't accept it."
Archie Bunker

"A bone to the dog is not charity. Charity is the bone shared with the dog, when you are just as hungry as the dog."
Jack London

COMMUNITY

"No man is an island, entire of itself; every man is a piece of the continent, a part of the main."

John Donne

"The good particular men may do separately . . . is small compared with what they may do collectively."

Benjamin Franklin

"Survival of the fittest may be a good working description of the process of evolution, but a government of humans should elevate itself to a higher order, one which tries to fill the cruel gaps left by chance and by a wisdom that we don't fully understand."

Mario Cuomo

"Alone, we can do so little; together, we can do so much."

Helen Keller

DIPLOMACY

"What is the good of a treaty? Aren't all human beings natural allies already? And if a person's prepared to ignore a fundamental bond like that, is he likely to pay much attention to a mere form of words?"

Thomas More

"Nations have no permanent friends, only permanent interests."

Robert Stewart

"Personal diplomacy and relationship-building, although important, are rarely the paramount drivers of global affairs. These are shaped importantly by the long-term national interest."

Henry A. Kissinger

"Negotiation in the classic diplomatic sense assumes parties more anxious to agree than to disagree."

Dean Acheson

"At first glance, the idea of sitting down with adversaries seems hard to quarrel with, but negotiation is not a policy. It is a technique. Saying that one favors negotiation has no more intellectual content than saying one favors using a spoon. For what? Under what circumstances? With what objectives? Like all human activity, negotiation has costs and benefits. If only benefits were involved, then it would be hard to quarrel with the 'What can we lose?' mantra one hears so often. In fact, the costs and potential downsides are real, and not to be ignored."

John Bolton

"It is the availability of raw power, not the use of it, that makes for effective diplomacy."

Edmund Morris, in *The Rise of Theodore Roosevelt*

"The philosopher deals with truth; the statesman addresses contingencies. The thinker has a duty to define what is right; the policymaker must deal with what is attainable. The professor focuses on ultimate goals; the diplomat knows that his is a meandering path on which there are few ultimate solutions and whatever 'solutions' there are, more often than not turn into a threshold for a new set of problems."

Henry A. Kissinger

"If you are prepared to give everything away to your opponent, you can usually get him to sign a piece of paper."
Jonathan S. Tobin

EDUCATION

"Civilization is a race between education and catastrophe."
H. G. Wells

"If you are thinking a year ahead, sow seed. If you are thinking ten years ahead, plant a tree. If you are thinking one hundred years ahead, educate the people."
Guan Zhong

"The battle of Waterloo was won on the playing fields of Eton."
Arthur Wellesley

"To defend a country you need an army, but to defend a civilization you need education."
Jonathan Sacks

"A child's education should begin at least one hundred years before he is born."
Oliver Wendell Holmes, Sr.

"Democracy needs to be reborn in every generation and education is its midwife."
John Dewey

"[E]ducation among all kinds of men always has had, and always will have, an element of danger and revolution, of dissatisfaction and discontent. Nevertheless, men strive to know."
W. E. B. Du Bois

"Education is not the filling of a pail, but the lighting of a fire."
  William Butler Yeats

"A child miseducated is a child lost."
  John F. Kennedy

EQUALITY

"Equality is inspiring as a legal ideal, stifling as a social reality."
  Thomas Szasz

"The law, in its majestic equality, forbids the rich as well as the poor to sleep under bridges, to beg in the streets, and to steal bread."
  Anatole France

"The emphasis on reservations and quotas as the most effective means of promoting affirmative action flies in the face of the constitutional provisions in favor of equal opportunity and equality under the law. It is never easy to reconcile 'special opportunities for some' with 'equal opportunity for all.'"
  Shashi Tharoor

"On a legal issue, I think a wise old woman and a wise old man are going to reach the same conclusion. But having the American people look at the court and think of it as being fair and appropriate for our nation, it helps to have women, plural, on the court."
  U.S. Supreme Court Justice *Sandra Day O'Connor*

"As women gain rights, families flourish, and so do societies. That connection is built on a simple truth: Whenever you include a group that's been excluded, you benefit everyone. And when you're working globally to include women and girls, who are half of every population, you're working to benefit all members of every community. Gender equity lifts everyone. Women's rights and society's health and wealth rise together."

Melinda Gates

"There is always inequality in life. Some men are killed in war and some men are wounded, and some men never leave the country, and some men are stationed in the Antarctic and some are stationed in San Francisco. It's very hard in military or in personal life to assure complete equality. Life is unfair."

John F. Kennedy

FREEDOM

"The only freedom which deserves the name is that of pursuing our own good in our own way, so long as we do not attempt to deprive others of theirs, or impede their efforts to obtain it. Each is the proper guardian of his own health, whether bodily, or mental and spiritual."

John Stuart Mill

"It is seldom that liberty of any kind is lost all at once. Slavery has so frightful an aspect to men accustomed to freedom that it must steal in upon them by degrees and must disguise itself in a thousand different shapes in order to be received."

David Hume

"When a man is denied the right to live the life he believes in, he has no choice but to become an outlaw."

Nelson Mandela

"When liberty dies in the hearts of people, no constitution and no laws will save it."

Learned Hand

"If a nation values anything more than freedom, it will lose its freedom; and the irony of it is that if it is comfort or money that it values more, it will lose that too."

Somerset Maugham

"Find out just what any people will quietly submit to and you have found out the exact measure of injustice and wrong which will be imposed upon them, and these will continue till they are resisted with either words or blows, or with both. The limits of tyrants are prescribed by the endurance of those whom they oppress."

Frederick Douglass

HUMAN RIGHTS

"The rights of every man are diminished when the rights of one man are threatened."

John F. Kennedy

"A government that tramples on the rights of its citizens denies the purpose of its existence."

Henry A. Kissinger

"The test of a society is not whether violations of human rights occasionally occur, but how they are dealt with by the authorities."

Alan M. Dershowitz

"Crimes do not cease to be criminal because they have a political motive."

Hartley Shawcross

IMMIGRANTS

"We are and always will be a nation of immigrants. We were strangers once, too."

Barack Obama

"The American experiment of self-government was an experiment statistically skewed from the outset, because it wasn't the people with sociable genes who fled the crowded Old World for the new continent; it was the people who didn't get along well with others."

Jonathan Franzen

"The happy and powerful do not go into exile."

Alexis de Tocqueville

JUSTICE AND INJUSTICE

"Injustice anywhere is a threat to justice everywhere. We are caught in an inescapable network of mutuality, tied in a single garment of destiny. Whatever affects one directly, affects all indirectly."

Martin Luther King, Jr.

"A defendant is entitled to a fair trial but not a perfect one."

Sherman Minton

"There can be no equal justice where the kind of trial a man gets depends on the money he has."

Hugo Black

"[T]he chief problem in any community cursed with crime is not punishment of the criminals, but the preventing of the young from being trained to crime."

W. E. B. Du Bois

"A man's head is not like a scallion, which will grow again if you cut it off; if you cut it off wrongly, then even if you want to correct your error, there is no way of doing it."

Mao Zedong

LAW

"The law is always too short and too tight for growing humankind. The best you can do is somethin' and then make up some law to fit and by the time that law gets on the books, you'd have done somethin' different."

Robert Penn Warren, in *All the King's Men*

"The life of the law has not been logic; it has been experience. The felt necessities of the time . . . avowed or unconscious . . . have had a good deal more to do than the syllogism in determining the rules by which men should be governed."

Oliver Wendell Holmes, Jr.

"The reason we have laws at all is not so 'good' people can impose their will on 'bad' people, but because everyone has the capacity to do bad things."

James Taranto

"A wall protecting a pasture, however vast the pasture, defines the limits of that pasture. And any definition of a right, however sweeping, sets limits to that right."

George F. Will

"Don't ever get caught up in the criminal justice system. As soon as you're caught in the machinery, just the machinery, you've lost. The only question remaining is how much you're going to lose. Once you enter a cell—even before you've had a chance to declare your innocence—you become a cipher. There is no more you."

Tom Wolfe, in *Bonfire of the Vanities*

"When there is a popular will, there is a rabbinic way."

Blu Greenberg

"There are not enough jails, not enough police, not enough courts to enforce a law not supported by the people."

Hubert H. Humphrey

LEARNING

"Education is not like a decal, to be slipped off a piece of stiff paper and pasted on the back of the skull. The point of education is to waken innocent minds to a suspicion of information."

Russell Baker

"Tell me and I'll forget. Show me and I'll remember. Involve me and I'll understand."

Benjamin Franklin

"Do not say, 'When I have leisure, I will study,' for you may never have leisure."

Hillel, in *Teachings of the Fathers*

"Love of a subject is a better teacher than a sense of duty."

Albert Einstein

"The beautiful thing about learning is that no one can take it away from you."

B. B. King

"When you talk, you are only repeating what you already know. But if you listen, you may learn something new."

Dalai Lama

MORALITY

"Morality isn't a question of result but of intent."

Yaakov Lozowick

"Where nothing is unspeakable, nothing is undoable."

Alexander Bickel

"For what reason, barring Original Sin, is a man most likely to step over the line? Ambition, love, fear, money."

Robert Penn Warren, in *All the King's Men*

"If you do the right thing and lose, you still did the right thing. If you do less than the right thing and win, it's morally reprehensible."

Tom Coburn

PEACE

"Peace is purchased from strength."

Benjamin Netanyahu

"There was never a peace made, however advantageous, that was not condemned as weakness and its makers censured as injudicious or corrupt."

Benjamin Franklin

"Peace, if it ever exists, will not be based on the fear of war, but on the love of peace. It will not be the abstaining from an act, but the coming of a state of mind. In this sense the most insignificant writer can serve peace, where the most powerful tribunals can do nothing."

Julien Benda

"They make a desert and call it peace."

Tacitus

"Peace at any price isn't peace; it's surrender."

Eric Cantor

"There is no final victory of peace. It must be won again and again, generation after generation, through the dedication, sacrifice, and perseverance of a free citizenry."

Tom Daschle

"Better the pains of peace than the agonies of war."

Yitzhak Rabin

"I destroy my enemies when I make them my friends."

Abraham Lincoln

"If you want to make peace, you don't talk to your friends. You talk to your enemies."

Moshe Dayan

"You cannot shake hands with a clenched fist."

Indira Gandhi

PROGRESS

"Even a little bit better is better."
Minna Berchin

"It staggers the imagination to think of the endless efforts that must have been expended in the first domestication of animals, in the discovery of planting seed, in the first working of surface ores. It is only because man is a socially cooperative creature that he has succeeded in perpetuating himself at all."
Robert L. Heilbroner

"It's not madness which turns the world upside down, it's conscience."
Bernard Malamud

"Incumbents very seldom invent the future."
Eric Schmidt

"Never doubt that a small group of thoughtful, committed citizens can change the world. Indeed, it's the only thing that ever has."
Margaret Mead

PUBLIC SERVICE

"There is no cause half so sacred as the cause of a people. There is no idea so uplifting as the idea of service to humanity."
Woodrow Wilson

"Be ashamed to die until you have won some victory for humanity."
Horace Mann

"One must repeat, from time to time: 'The world was created for my sake.' Never say: 'What do I care about this or that?' Do your part to add something new, to bring forth something that is needed, and to leave the world a little better because you were here briefly."

Nachman of Bratzlav

"You can find meaning in life only by commitment to great goals; self-service may purchase the goods in the supermarket, but in life purchases disillusionment and despair."

Frank H. T. Rhodes

"Life is an exciting business and most exciting when it is lived for others."

Helen Keller

"The sacrifice of life is, in many cases, the easiest of all sacrifices. Many youths fail to understand that to sacrifice five or six years of their seething youth to hard and tedious study, if only to multiply ten-fold their powers of serving the truth and the cause they have set before them as their goal, is utterly beyond the strength of many of them."

Fyodor Dostoyevsky, in *The Brothers Karamazov*

"My country is the world, and my religion is to do good."

Thomas Paine

"If you find faults with our country, make it a better one. If you're disappointed with the mistakes of government, join its ranks and work to correct them. Enlist in our Armed Forces. Become a teacher. Enter the ministry. Run for public office. Feed a hungry child. Teach an illiterate adult to read. Comfort the afflicted. Defend the rights of the oppressed. Our country will be the better, and you will be the happier—because nothing brings greater happiness in life than to serve a cause greater than yourself."

John McCain

"Ask not what your country can do for you, ask what you can do for your country."

John F. Kennedy

"Even an oft-repeated, mundane task takes on greater significance in the service of a lofty goal."

Ahuva Halberstam

"Happiness can only come from giving at least a corner of yourself to others. God help the person who goes through life doing nothing for someone else. He's doomed."

Theodore Hesburgh

"Nobody need wait a single moment before starting to improve the world."

Anne Frank

STRUGGLE

"The whole history of the progress of human liberty shows that all concessions yet made to her august claims have been born of earnest struggle. . . . If there is no struggle, there is no progress. Those who profess to favor freedom and yet deprecate agitation are like men who want crops without plowing up the ground, they want rain without thunder and lightning, and they want the ocean without the awful roar of its many waters."

Frederick Douglass

"No movement toward freedom has succeeded in the blink of an eye, absent a struggle, or without periods when all has seemed lost."
   Natan Sharansky

"Three hundred years of humiliation, abuse, and deprivation cannot be expected to find voice in a whisper."
   Martin Luther King, Jr.

"If you're not ready to die for it, put the word 'freedom' out of your vocabulary."
   Malcolm X

"One should never wear one's best trousers to go out and battle for freedom and truth."
   Henrik Ibsen

TEACHERS

"I am indebted to my father for living, but to my teacher for living well."
   Alexander the Great

"It is the personality of the teacher which is the text that the pupils read, the text that they will never forget."
   Abraham Joshua Heschel

"Technology is just a tool. In terms of getting the kids working together and motivating them, the teacher is the most important."
   Bill Gates

"I am not a teacher, but an awakener."
   Robert Frost

"Nine-tenths of education is encouragement."
  Anatole France

"A teacher affects eternity; he can never tell where his influence stops."
  Henry Adams

Index

A FEW WORDS ON TYPOGRAPHY

"Type well used is invisible as type, just as the perfect talking voice is the unnoticed vehicle for the transmission of words, ideas."
Beatrice Warde

While the quotations in *Other People's Words* are the reason for this book, as a longtime admirer and student of typefaces, I'm happy to share a few words about the fonts selected by Steven Seighman, the book's designer.

The main text has been set in Baskerville, a classic serif font created in the 1750s by successful businessman, John Baskerville. After working as a calligrapher and a gravestone engraver, Baskerville made a fortune in manufacturing, and turned his attention to the poor quality of printed books common in his time. Unhappy with typefaces then available, he decided to develop an artistic but functional approach to numbers and letters to enhance the reading experience. Although he didn't live to see wide acceptance of his graphic creation, Baskerville is used today in an array of alphabets and in more than ninety languages.

One great fan of Baskerville's work was the Italian printer, engraver, and graphic designer, Giambattista Bodoni. He used Baskerville as the starting point for his own 1790s serif typeface.

Bodoni's creation has also long survived, and has been the inspiration for many typeface designers, including in our era. In one form or another, Bodoni is widely seen in titles, logos, and posters. The typeface used for the category headings throughout the book (and also on the cover) is a very popular 1994 version of the original Bodoni called ITC [for International Typeface Corporation] Bodoni Seventy-Two.

Other People's Words was printed and bound in the United States. The paper for the first edition was #55 EarthChoice Book Antique Cream White.